MW00811501

The Perry's Camp Murders

Robert Allen

By R. S. Allen

with

Steve O. Watson

INFINITY
PUBLISHING.COM

Copyright © 2009 by R. S. Allen

All rights reserved. No part of this book shall be reproduced or transmitted in any form or by any means, electronic, mechanical, magnetic, photographic including photocopying, recording or by any information storage and retrieval system, without prior written permission of the publisher. No patent liability is assumed with respect to the use of the information contained herein. Although every precaution has been taken in the preparation of this book, the publisher and author assume no responsibility for errors or omissions. Neither is any liability assumed for damages resulting from the use of the information contained herein.

ISBN 0-7414-5528-5

Published by:

INFINITY
PUBLISHING.COM

1094 New DeHaven Street, Suite 100
West Conshohocken, PA 19428-2713
Info@buybooksontheweb.com
www.buybooksontheweb.com
Toll-free (877) BUY BOOK
Local Phone (610) 941-9999
Fax (610) 941-9959

Printed in the United States of America

Published August 2009

Dedicated to

The Families and Descendants of

Charles Perry, Josie Law, and

Luther "Bun" Ward

Table of Contents

Acknowledgments   vii

Special Acknowledgment   xi

Introduction   1

Chapter 1 – *The Milieu of Sevier County in 1949*   5

Chapter 2 – *The History of Perry's Camp*   11

Chapter 3 – *The Victims*   19

Chapter 4 – *The Crime Scene*   27

Chapter 5 – *The Investigation and the Motives*   38

Chapter 6 – *The Defendants*   48

Chapter 7 – *The Prior Conviction of Robertson in "Bun" Ward's Killing*   55

Chapter 8 – *The Trial*   63

Chapter 9 – *The Defense's Decision to Plead Their Clients*   81

Chapter 10 – *The Accounts of Detective Magazines*   84

Chapter 11 – *The Time Line –What Really Happened*   91

Chapter 12 – *The Post Trial Lives of the Defendants and Their Families*   **100**

Chapter 13 – *The Recollections of Sevier Countians*   **116**

Chapter 14 – *The Recollections of Mosey Moore's Nephews*   **126**

Chapter 15 – *The Similarities with the White Cap Murders*   **133**

Chapter 16 – *The Most Heinous Sevier County Crimes Since the Perry's Camp Murders*   **139**

Chapter 17 – *The Author's Observations and Conclusions*   **149**

Acknowledgments

Grateful acknowledgements are given to the following sources of documented information and photographs which made this book possible.

ancestry.com

answers.com

archive.southcoasttoday.com

Archives of *The Knoxville News-Sentinel* and
The Knoxville Journal

bulk.resource.org/courts.gov (U. S. v. Brady & Marshall)

Detective Cases, March 1958

dlc.lib.utk.edu

Vivian Law England

Federal Bureau of Prisons

Kingsport Times

Grainger County, Tennessee and Its People, 1998,
Walsworth Publishing

Jere Loveday

Agnes Marshall

Barbara McGill

Mission-Aider Newsletter of Holston Valley
Baptist Association, January 2008

Beth Beal O'Donnell

Pigeon Forge Public Library Genealogy

Real Detective, April 1950

Alfred C. Schmutzer, Jr.

"Scrapbook Clippings with Monroe County, Tennessee Ties"
by Joan B. Troy, tngenweb.org

Sevier County Library Genealogy

Sevier County Sheriff's Department

Sevier County, Tennessee and Its Heritage, 1994,
Walsworth Publishing

smokykin.com

Nancy Snipes

Tennessee Department of Corrections

tba.org/Journal ("The Rocky Top Murders" by
Donald F. Paine)

tsc.state.tn.us/OPINIONS (TN v. Michelle Tipton)

The Montgomery Vindicator

Timely Detective, March 1950

therogersvillereview.com

White Caps by Ethelred W. Crozier, 1899, Bean, Warters & Gaul Printers and Binders

Wikipedia, the free encyclopedia

Mrs. J. T. (Shirley) Wolfenbarger

Special Acknowledgment

The contributions of my friend and collaborator, Steve O. Watson, are especially acknowledged. Without his help, knowledge, and recollections this endeavor would have been even more difficult and time consuming. The crime scene photographs, the *Real Detective* account, his interviews of local Sevier Countians, and his personal experiences and remembrances rounded out my efforts and made them better and more complete. For all of that, I am forever grateful.

Introduction

Anyone alive in Sevier County, Tennessee in September 1949, young or old, town or country resident, heard about the Perry's Camp murders. Everyone learned all they could about what had happened. It was the kind of thing that just did not occur in Sevier County, not in those times. Such heinous crimes were as foreign as drug trafficking. They occurred in places like New York, Chicago, and Detroit, not in Sevier County. These acts of robbery, torture, and murder were forever etched into the minds of all those in all the county's communities – whether it be Sevierville, Pigeon Forge, Gatlinburg, Seymour, or Boogertown.

Among the Sevier County populace that learned all they could about these crimes were the author, a 6-year-old resident of Sevierville, and the author's collaborator, a 7-year-old resident of Boogertown, a mountain community located near Gatlinburg. Both their fathers followed local politics and knew those in office. Everyone knew J. Roy Whaley was the Sevier County Sheriff. Most people knew Bill Reagan, Chief of Police in Sevierville and Sevier County coroner. Their deputies and officers were known to most by their first names. Such men were in the public eye anyway but these well-publicized crimes made the badges pinned on their chests even more prominent. The Perry's Camp murders somehow seemed to escalate and enhance their standing in the community. A number of people also knew Charlie Perry, an allegedly reformed Knoxville bootlegger who had moved to Sevier County 20 years before

1

his death and built a successful tourist business between Pigeon Forge and Gatlinburg.

The author and collaborator would years later embark on law enforcement careers but this would be their first experience with homicide, with unspeakable tortuous acts, with premeditated murder. They learned that one of those arrested, who would be given a 99-year prison sentence, was from Sevier County. The author, whose best friend at the time was the killer's nephew, would learn years later his exact kinship to the murderer. Because of this and the fact that there was no trial or any public records detailing the evidence in these crimes, the author and his collaborator set out to re-establish the facts of this double homicide and robbery, frequently referred to at that time as the worst crimes to occur in Sevier County in over 50 years.

Because the only public records still available were the court records detailing charges and proceedings long since archived away in the county library, the best evidence concerning what actually occurred was the newspaper accounts, especially the accounts chronicling the short trial before the pleas were changed from not guilty to guilty. The second best accounts, but a distant second, were those contained in detective magazines of those days. An examination was conducted of these accounts and they were for the most part found to be embellished and fictionalized. In fact, if all the detective accounts were combined, one-third of the story would be factual, one-third embellished, and one-third fictional. Information was gathered from those elder citizens still living that had information of value to share. Unfortunately, some of those recollections proved to be the least reliable, but that's understandable since almost 60 years had passed. Some of the best information came from descendants of those that experienced tragedy first hand. And lastly, information was gleaned from written accounts of researchers, witnesses, and associates long since dead.

Aside from the details of the crimes and the resulting adjudications, this work also examines the lives and background of the victims and the perpetrators before September, 1949 as well as the lives of the killers after the abbreviated trial. The most intriguing part of the story may well be that which tells of the lives of the perpetrators after the crimes, their indictment, and conviction. Two were sentenced to 99 years while a third was acquitted and released. The three lived out their years in very different ways. Additionally, this story examines the impact of these crimes on the families of both the victims and the murderers. The story includes recollections from residents alive at the time the Perry's Camp murders occurred and concludes with comparisons to other murders that occurred 50 years before and during the half century following.

Chapter 1

The Milieu of Sevier County in 1949

The Sevier County of 1949 was a world apart from the Sevier County of today—a tourist Mecca that millions visit annually. There were no go-cart tracks, water slides, theaters with live shows, wedding chapels, bungee jumps, or helicopter rides. There were few hotels and restaurants in any part of the county other than Gatlinburg where the tourism industry was growing into adolescence. The other two towns—Pigeon Forge and especially Sevierville, the county seat, were showing only limited signs of interest in the tourist trade. Even Rebel Railroad in Pigeon Forge, which would eventually evolve into Dollywood, did not yet exist.

Sevier County was still primarily a farming community as evidenced by the fields of corn and tobacco patches that lined the fertile river bottom land on both sides of the highway in Pigeon Forge. Sevierville was the county's commerce center—both retail and banking—which further proof of the county's agricultural roots. One could hardly walk a straight line down the sidewalks of Sevierville on Saturdays for the people. Saturday was the day the farmers and their families came to town to shop. As a kid it was almost as difficult to walk the Saturday sidewalks in Sevierville without getting sprayed with tobacco juice as it was to simply go from one place to another. Because farming was the most common vocation in the county, people worked five days a week from sunrise to sunset, shopped on Saturday, and went to church on Sunday.

The creation of the Great Smoky Mountain National Park in 1934 had resulted in Gatlinburg being dubbed "The Gateway" to the Park and had prompted its growth toward tourism to escalate. The Park also limited Gatlinburg's growth as the Park bounded the city on three sides. In years to come this would cause the growth in Pigeon Forge and Sevierville to accelerate at a faster rate.

Of course, this growth was stunted for a time because of the lack of sufficient roads. There was only one four-lane highway in Sevier County in 1949 and that was Chapman Highway (U. S. Highway 441) which connected Sevierville to Knoxville. Not only was Interstate 40 twenty years away from completion there was no four-lane highway connecting Sevierville, Pigeon Forge, and Gatlinburg. It would take the entire decade of the 1950's for this to be accomplished. The road system was starting to be strained at times but in 1949 it was adequate to handle the weekend sightseers visiting the Park and the family vacationers and honeymooners visiting Gatlinburg during the tourist season. The "tourist season" in 1949 Gatlinburg kicked off with Memorial Day and ended with the last car that left on Labor Day morning. By Labor Day afternoon a cannon could have been fired down the center of the parkway in Gatlinburg without hitting anyone.

The following photographs better depict the milieu of Sevier County at the time of the Perry's Camp murders than any words. The first photograph shows the parkway at Middle Creek Road (Old Mill Avenue) in Pigeon Forge at the intersection where traffic light #7 now hangs. Only the northbound lane was paved and was being utilized as a two-lane road handling both north and south-bound traffic. The south-bound side of the parkway had been graded, but none of it was yet paved. The largest white building at the left was Ward-Beal Garage which was located on what is now River Road. The white end building facing the parkway on the right was Large's Food Market and service station; next to it was Watson's grocery and restaurant; next to Watson's was

6

Trotter's Electric and Plumbing; and on the back corner was Butler's General Merchandise, depicted in the second photograph. On the other side of the Little Pigeon River (evidenced by the tree-line) was the Pigeon Forge landmark—the Old Mill.

"Downtown" Pigeon Forge and the Parkway in 1950

Butler's General Merchandise

The permanent population of Sevier County in the 1940s and 1950s was 23,300 people, give or take a few. In 2000 the population was just over 71,000. The 2010 population is estimated at 87,000. Some 10 million people now visit the Park annually.

Life in 1949 Sevier County was easy going and simple. People worked, raised families, and went to church. The county was small enough that people in Sevierville knew people in Pigeon Forge and Gatlinburg as well as in communities in between. The Sevier County Sheriff had 3-4 deputies and the police chiefs in Sevierville, Pigeon Forge, and Gatlinburg had even fewer men. People felt safe and secure in their homes. Front doors were seldom locked. It really was a different time and place.

Professional law enforcement in the county was in its infancy. The leading and most powerful law enforcement officer in the county, of course, was the sheriff, an elected official. When additional manpower was needed beyond what he and his few deputies could manage, he had to turn to local police departments, constables, also elected officials, and the Tennessee Highway Patrol (THP). The Sevier County Sheriff's Department, as well as any other sheriff's departments in the state, would not have been nearly as effective without the assistance of the THP. The Tennessee Bureau of Investigation (TBI), originally known as the Tennessee Bureau of Criminal Identification (TBCI), would not be created until March, 1951. Crimes in Sevier County with the exception of domestic disputes were non-violent and most frequently were either property crimes or related to the manufacture and distribution of non-tax paid liquor (moonshine whiskey). Violent crime was more prevalent in Cocke County than Sevier County.

The sheriff of Sevier County in 1949 was J. Roy Whaley who had been elected to his fourth 2-year term the previous year. Whaley, 40 years of age in 1949, would serve one more term before becoming a U. S. Deputy Marshall in Knoxville in 1953.

All the things that made up Sevier County in 1949— farming, growing tourism in Gatlinburg, Saturday shopping in Sevierville, proposed road construction, elections—all contributed to perhaps the favorite pastime of most adult males in the county—"politicking." This was a popular hobby most any day of the week but was most prevalent on Saturdays on the courthouse lawn and the surrounding sidewalks. Dolly Parton's statue now occupies a prime location on the front lawn of the courthouse. The statue displaced space occupied by hundreds of politicking huddles over the years before it was built.

The main event of politicking was, of course, the general election held every two years in August. Primary elections were unneeded. Bipartisan politics didn't exist in Sevier County then; everybody was Republican. The culmination of these contests occurred on election night on the courthouse steps when the tallies would be recorded periodically on a large easel type blackboard as the votes were being counted. Most contests would be decided by midnight but close races would sometimes wear on into the early morning hours before a winner could be comfortably declared.

Things were very different during this time. Most homes had a free-standing cabinet style radio but black and white televisions were still a few years away. Electricity had come to the county after construction of Douglas Dam, located nine miles from Sevierville on the French Broad River. The Tennessee Valley Authority completed the dam in February, 1943. Telephones were not in every home and this luxury was still so new that some two-digit phone numbers still existed and party lines were common place.

Douglas Dam

This was Sevier County in 1949. This was the way things were. This was the setting for one of the most heinous crimes of the century.

Chapter 2

The History of Perry's Camp

Perry's Camp emerged from Flat Branch Hollow between 1928 and 1935. It included a two-story log and stone building with a restaurant on the first floor and living quarters on the second floor and eleven tourist cabins that stretched from the mouth of the hollow, across Highway 71 (Gatlinburg Highway), to the other side of the west prong of the Little Pigeon River. The cabins were of similar construction and were built during the same time period as the main building except one near the dam on the east bank of the river. This cabin was converted from an old mill. Perry's Camp was located at Flat Branch Road and Highway 71 three miles north of downtown Gatlinburg and was developed by Charles J. Perry, a Knoxville bootlegger who bought his first piece of property in Flat Branch Hollow in 1928.

Perry's purpose in buying up additional parcels of property in Flat Branch Hollow and the surrounding vicinity was to develop it for tourism. He obviously was a man of some vision as he recognized the area's potential. He started Perry's Camp two years after LeConte Lodge had been built on Mount LeConte in the Smokies and a half dozen years before the Park was officially established. Gatlinburg's first hotel, the Mountain View Hotel, had been built in 1916, enlarged and remodeled, and then torn down in 1929 to allow for construction of the new Mountain View Hotel in 1930.

Of the eleven cabins, five were located to the rear of a house on the property, which dated back to 1850, and which separated the restaurant building from these cabins. A sixth cabin was east of the house while the remaining five were on the banks of the river, two on the west side and three on the east side. Those three cabins were accessible only by a swinging bridge. There was no road on the east side of the river. This meant that guests in any of those cabins had to carry their luggage across the swinging bridge after checking in, and back again when checking out.

Perry's Camp 1942

Perry created attractions outside and inside the restaurant building. A revenuer-disabled moonshine still greeted visitors as they pulled into the parking lot. There was a water wheel to the rear of the building which, through a series of pulleys and belts, powered a ceiling fan in the dining room. And perhaps the most eye-catching of all was a bar made of a hollowed-out poplar log lined with copper and covered with a glass top. Small fish swam in spring water piped into one end with the excess flowing back into Flat Branch which ran under the building. Bar stools attached to the floor ran the full length of the bar. Such gimmicks sparked the interest of Perry's visitors and encouraged them to stay or to visit again.

The Water Wheel

The Still

These features and others were described by "Ev" (Everett Charles) Whaley of Pigeon Forge to Mack Trotter Marshall, known as "Little Mack" to family and friends, who bought Perry's Camp in 1952. Ev had worked for Charlie Perry as a cook and "jack of all trades" on and off during the 20 years that Perry's Camp existed. In June 1990, six years before his death, "Little Mack" recorded and transcribed a conversation with Ev who was 81 at the time and who died seven years later. The conversation took place at Marshall's home which was previously a part of Perry's Camp. Whaley talked about a number of enlightening aspects about Perry's Camp and Perry.

Dam, Power House, Swinging Bridge, and Josie Law
May, 1937

14

Whaley told Marshall that just about everything at Perry's Camp—the restaurant building, the cabins, the dam across the river, the power house on the other side of the river used to generate power for the camp—most everything—was built for Perry by "Vic" Marshall (no relation to Mack) of Pigeon Forge. Most of the unique ideas and features of Perry's Camp originated with Perry whom Whaley described as an "armchair engineer." In addition to the dam, the swinging bridge, water wheel, and bar, a man-made cave was dug into the side of the hill to serve as the garage for Perry's 1928 Buick.

Perhaps the most unique and secretive features at Perry's Camp were the spaces created to hide home brew and liquor during the time beer was not legal. The home-made stuff was hidden in the water wheel, hollow porch posts at the rear of the restaurant, and hollow exterior stone steps. Ev commented, "I made five gallons of home brew every day, and capped it, and we sold it for 25 cents a bottle." Whaley talked about how he had packed coins into quart jars, joking that the Sevierville gang that bought most of the home brew usually paid with silver, not currency. Whaley never knew where Perry hid the money jars.

Ev mentioned other revelations to Mack. Ev stated "He had a beautiful log cabin, built by Vic Marshall, and if I get the story right, there used to be a beautiful little church here, called Cardwell's Chapel, sit right where the building was...And that burnt down in about—somewhere in—twenty-eight or nine, early twenty-nine. My dad's opinion was that Charlie Perry got old John Quarrels (also spelled Quarles) to burn that little church down—and my dad said, 'Now, you just wait and see, something will happen to old Perry worse than that,' said 'now, you just don't burn down church houses and get by with it.' And sure enough, it did happen—later on—several years later."

Marshall, during the course of his conversation with Whaley, acknowledged that he had heard the same allegation concerning Quarles from two separate sources, but neither of them had offered any definitive proof. Whaley responded, "That's what they assumed. Yeah. Didn't have no evidence, but...Yeah, but the building and stuff started right away after that happened, and..."

Cardwell's Chapel was a church that had been moved from Gatlinburg three miles away in 1914 to Flat Branch property owned by Robert Cardwell. This was done as a matter of convenience for the church's members, many of whom had relocated to the Flat Branch community. James Cardwell, Robert's father, had years before donated the land for the church in Gatlinburg.

In December 1991 Mack and his wife, Agnes, interviewed Lucinda Oakley Ogle, the "Queen of the Smoky Mountains," a woman every bit the icon of mountain heritage that Dolly Parton is of mountain singing, at her Gatlinburg home. Ms. Ogle, who packed more knowledge and information of mountain living and Sevier County into her life of 94 years that ended in 2003 than anyone else, was always willing to share her knowledge and her stories. Among the subjects discussed with the Marshalls was Cardwell's Chapel. Among comments made by Ms. Ogle about Perry was, "He wanted to do away with the church but they had—they had—well, it burned down. We always thought, maybe, he had it burned." Ms. Ogle recalled it was in the parking lot of that church, used by young people to park and spark, that she decided to marry her husband, Earnest Ogle, on November 17, 1926. She reminisced about that day, the sadness she felt after the church burned, and the terrible tragedy that occurred there years later.

In August 1992 Mack and Agnes Marshall recorded and transcribed an interview of Cora Ownby Morton, age 88, who died in 1996, along with her son, Reverend Henry Albert Morton, age 56, who died four months following the interview. Ms. Morton was born in the Flat Branch (Perry's

Camp) community, moved from there to the Glades community of Gatlinburg as a child but remained extremely knowledgeable about the Flat Branch area. During this interview the Mortons unexpectedly disclosed that William "Bill" Conway Quarles, husband of Mrs. Morton's cousin, Mae Cardwell, shortly before his death in 1950, confessed to burning down Cardwell's Chapel in 1930. Bill Quarles, brother of John Quarles, burned down the church so Perry would buy the church property and his property which he wanted to sell. Perry wanted the Quarles' property but would not buy it by itself because of its close proximity to the church. That close proximity would have prevented Perry from obtaining a beer license.

Following the settlement of Perry's estate in 1950, Cliff Davis, a local Sevierville businessman bought Perry's Camp and operated it for a couple of years. The restaurant was transformed into a gift shop so the kitchen was used very little. When Mack and Agnes Marshall bought Perry's Camp from Davis in 1952 the blood stain on the kitchen floor where Perry had been murdered three years before remained. The Marshalls cleaned the kitchen and painted over the stain as they operated it for a time as a restaurant once again.

The November 2, 1950 edition of *The Montgomery Vindicator*, Sevierville's weekly newspaper contained an article and an advertisement of the auction of the personal property of the C. J. Perry estate set for Friday, November 4th at Perry's Camp. The auction ad announced the sale of "hundreds & hundreds of items" including electric utilities, restaurant and office equipment, tourist cabin furniture, an automobile and truck, shop and power tools, building supplies, farm and garden tools, and other personal properties. The administrator of the estate was identified as Xan C. Davenport and the auctioneers as Sarten & Allen of Sevierville.

In the late '50's the Gatlinburg Spur of the Foothills Parkway (U. S. Highway 441), a 4.6 mile stretch of road between Gatlinburg and Pigeon Forge, was constructed. This spur consists of two 2-lane highways—the southbound on the west side of the river and the northbound on the east side. This project required the state acquisition of substantial amounts of land on both sides of the river. The end result for Perry's Camp, or Flat Branch Court as it was then called, was the loss of the restaurant building, six cabins, other out buildings, the swinging bridge, and the dam.

The Marshalls, based on the suggestion of one of Mack's professors at the University of Tennessee, initially renamed Perry's Camp MacAg Cottages. They soon decided they really didn't care for that name and renamed the tourist court Flat Branch Court, then later, Flat Branch Cottages. On October 30, 1992 Perry's Camp was placed on The National Register of Historic Places. The listing includes the terracing, the rock walls, the four cabins, all built by Perry, and the 1850 log and rock house. These features of Perry's Camp, as well as the water wheel, the still, and the fan still exist today. Additionally, the chestnut boards, a rare commodity today, which had been nailed to the walls in Perry's restaurant were salvaged and used to renovate the walls of the 1850 house. Three of the four remaining cabins are still rented six months out of the year between May and November.

The National Register Plaque

18

Chapter 3

The Victims

Charlie Perry, born Charles Jackson Perry on August 4, 1879, died 45 days after his 70th birthday. He was buried in Fort Hill Cemetery, Cleveland, Tennessee with his parents, a brother and a sister. He was survived by two brothers, both of Chattanooga, and two sisters, one of Chattanooga and the other of Rock Springs, Georgia.

The first account of Perry was found in the 1909 Knoxville city directory which means he in all likelihood came to Knoxville from Cleveland in late 1908 when he was 29 years of age. He was employed as a clerk by Hugh Coleman, who had a soft drinks business at 622 East Jackson Avenue, and he lived in a rooming house at 719 McMillan. Between 1910 and 1913 Perry was employed at the same soft drinks business on East Jackson but lived at 906 Brigham Avenue. His whereabouts could not be accounted for between 1914 and 1916. In 1917 Perry worked at a garage at 419 West Depot Avenue and lived in a rooming house at 209 East Park Avenue.

It is believed that it was during the time he was working at the soft drinks business that he met and began a relationship with Maye Lawson McGhee who during that time was employed as a stenographer at C. M. McClung & Company, the largest wholesale and mail-order supplier of hardware, stoves, and other goods in Knoxville, also located on Jackson Avenue. Miss McGhee started working at C. M.

McClung in 1903 and was there for 10 years, all the while living with a Margaret McGhee at 300 East Park Avenue, a house owned by another McGhee family member, and less than a block from Perry's 1917 residence.

Maye Lawson McGhee came from well-known wealthy roots. Her great uncle was John McClung McGhee, one of the wealthiest businessmen in Knoxville, who, in the early 1880's, donated $40,000 for construction of the Knox County Library. The library was dedicated in 1884 and named Lawson McGhee Library in honor of his daughter, May Lawson McGhee Williams, who had died the year before during childbirth. Charles McClung McGhee and Calvin M. McClung of C. M. McClung Company were first cousins.

Maye Lawson McGhee had a younger sister, Alva, who married Thomas Calloway Howard in 1892. Maye Lawson McGhee's affair with Howard resulted in John McGhee (her father) and Joe McGhee (her brother) killing Howard's two brothers and a cousin in Monroe County in 1898. The McGhees were convicted in the first trial but were acquitted in the second trial. The first shooting led to a second, which occurred at the time of the second trial in Madisonville. By that time Lawson's sister and Tom Howard had divorced, and Lawson and Tom had married and moved to Knoxville. Howard, another brother, and an uncle showed up for the trial and encountered John and Joe McGhee and three other male family members. Shooting again broke out but only one man was killed, this being Charles Jones, John McGhee's son-in-law. Tom Howard was the shooter, and even though Jones was unarmed, the grand jury refused to indict Howard, declaring Jones had gotten in the way of the fray while Howard was acting in self-defense. Two years later, in 1902, Jones' brother and son gunned down Tom Howard on the street in Knoxville, shooting him six times before he could draw his gun. The Jones claimed self-defense and the jury agreed; both were acquitted. These events ended the feud but made for sensational headlines that were dredged up anytime the McGhee or Jones families made the news. Ironically, her life with Tom Howard ended in the same part of town, Jackson Avenue and Gay Street, where her life with Charles Perry began.

This Maye Lawson McGhee, who took back her maiden name following the death of Tom Howard, born February 17, 1878 in Monroe County, and Charles Jackson Perry eloped to Sevier County and were married by a Justice of the Peace on August 6, 1918. A month and a half later Perry, as required by all men born between September 11, 1872 and September 12, 1900, registered for the draft at Colbert County, Alabama. At that time, although he recorded his home address as R.F.D. No. 6, Knoxville, Tennessee, he reflected his employment as that of "Pipe Covering" at Nitrate Plate #1 at Sheffield, Alabama. His nearest relative was recorded as Mrs. Maye L. Perry of the same Knoxville address. Nitrate Plant #1 was one of three such plants built by the Army Corps of Engineers in the Muscle Shoals area to produce ammonium nitrate for explosives during World War I.

Charles and Lawson Perry apparently returned to Knoxville sometime between 1919 and 1921, and Perry opened an "eating house" called Perry's Lunch Room on Western Avenue near Henley Street. He and Lawson lived on Rutledge Pike. They remained together until about 1927 when Charles moved into an apartment and Lawson returned to Monroe County. Charles Perry remained in Knoxville until 1929 when he moved to Sevier County. Charles and Lawson divorced sometime thereafter and neither ever remarried although the common law marriage of Perry and Josie was recognized in the settling of their estates. In 1950 following Charlie's murder, Lawson received a note from her niece's husband, Barney Ray, telling her that Perry's Camp had sold at auction for a third of its worth. Upon her return to Monroe County, Lawson lived with her sisters,

Alva McGhee Howard and Miss Mayme Sue "Aunt Jack" McGhee, and Alva's daughter, Ailene "Boss" Howard. She was buried Mrs. Lawson McGhee Perry when she died January 8, 1951.

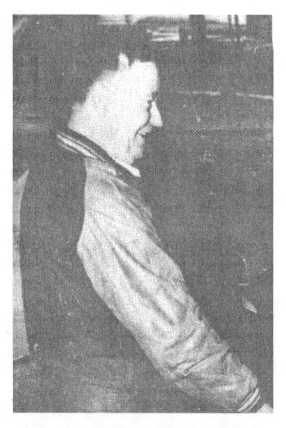

Charles J. Perry

Perry was a known bootlegger to the Knoxville Police Department and had arrests in 1927 for storing whiskey and for storing home brew and in 1928 for drunk and disorderly conduct. He was known to the Knoxville Police Department for a couple of other reasons as well. Perry had been involved in a shooting incident outside his café with a Knoxville police officer. Perry was hit in the wrist, and the officer was hit in the chest but both recovered fully. In addition, in 1934 the American Clothing Company in Knoxville was burglarized and $15,000 worth of clothing was taken. Perry tipped Knox County Sheriff Department detectives that two men had put the clothing in one of the cabins at Perry's Camp and were planning on moving the loot to North Carolina. The cabin was searched with Perry's consent and the clothing was recovered. Perry's tip led to three convictions. There was no indication that Perry was involved in the burglary, and he was never charged. Perry had no criminal record in Sevier County.

When Mack Marshall interviewed Ev Whaley in 1990 Whaley acknowledged to Marshall that Perry had killed a man while living in Knoxville. Ev stated, "Yeah, he shot him. He told me about killing him. Says, 'I had 'em down and he had a knife—he slashed me once—like to got my throat—I had my gun in my hand—I shot him in the head—his head just bounced off that concrete.'" When Marshall asked why Perry killed the man, Ev responded, "They was in together on the boot-legging somehow or other—he said. He said, 'he cheated me out of my—he was selling liquor for me—in the joint there…"

No other information was found about this case of apparent self-defense which occurred sometime during the 1920's. The only cases publicized by the Knoxville Police Department at the time of Perry's death were the arrests in 1927 and 1928 and the investigation regarding the American Clothing theft and subsequent recovery. No information was released pertaining to his killing a man, self-defense or otherwise.

Perry never married his live-in housekeeper, Josie Law, but they lived together as husband and wife for several years. He and Miss Law, called Jo by family and friends, were referred to as Mr. and Mrs. Perry by friends and neighbors. There was either an assumption they were married or those close to them preferred to assume they were married. Their relationship, however, was recognized as a common law marriage and since it was determined Josie preceded Perry in death, her estate was placed with his and sold together. Josie's family received nothing of her personal property. No information was developed indicating that anyone in Sevier County knew about Perry's marriage to Maye Lawson McGhee.

Perry had been successful at Perry's Camp and was known to have accumulated some money. It was rumored that he didn't believe in banks but that rumor turned out to be false as he had an account at the Bank of Sevierville at the time of his death.

There was a story that circulated through the Sevier County Sheriff's Department following Perry's death that he had always bought shoes for the students at nearby McCookville School every fall. Allegedly he would go to the teacher and get the shoe sizes of all the students who needed shoes, buy the shoes, and deliver them to the teacher for distribution.

Miss Law, born Josephine Emeline Law on June 8, 1906 in Cades Cove in Blount County, a small, petite woman, was 43 when she died. She was survived by one brother and one sister. Her mother had died five years earlier. She was laid to rest in Christy Hill Cemetery at Mountain View Church of Christ near Montvale Springs in Blount County. She remained at Rawlings-Miller Funeral Home in Sevierville for two days before being taken to Blount County for burial. A total of 147 mourners paid their respects at the Sevierville funeral home.

Josie Law met Charlie Perry sometime between 1927 and 1929 in Knoxville during the time that he still owned his Western Avenue business. She had left her Blount County home because of a physically abusive father. She was in her early 20's and Perry was almost 50. She is believed to have met Perry as the result of going to work for him. However their paths crossed, their paths united and remained together for over 20 years—until the day they died together. She moved with Perry to Sevier County and worked as his housekeeper after he got Perry's Camp up and going.

Josie Law at Age 20

Miss Law, like Perry, also married once. In June 1937 she married Avery Brownlow Ownby, Sr. of the nearby Caney Branch area and divorced him in October 1938 alleging abandonment. Ownby was in military service during the time they were married. Avery had been married once previously and married a third time after being divorced from Josie Law. She had a child, a girl, but gave the infant to an unknown relative to rear. Close examination of the photograph of Josie on the swinging bridge taken in May, 1937 in the first chapter suggests she was 5-6 months pregnant. The father of her child was unknown. Josie was afraid to keep the baby and rear it at Perry's Camp as she was deathly afraid of a man whom she believed would harm or take the baby if he found her. The assumption was that this man was the child's father. She relied on Perry for protection and was confident he would afford her the necessary protection if the need arose. Josie was very secretive about her personal life and her past.

Chapter 4

The Crime Scene

Jack Adams, the 17-year-old employee of Charles Perry who lived nearby, arrived at work as usual that Monday morning. The "Perry's Camp" neon sign was still on and the front door to the restaurant was open but he found no one astir. The tourist court had had only one cabin rented the night before, one back up on the hill to the rear of the restaurant and the house, a honeymoon couple from Kentucky, but their car was gone. Adams was reluctant about going upstairs where Perry and Miss Law slept, uncomfortable about intruding on their privacy. Adams walked to the other side of the river to see if Perry was over there but saw no sign of him. When he returned he sat down in the front porch swing to wait and snooze a little.

A couple of hours had passed when the Swan's bread truck driver, Marshall Cox, arrived to make his delivery. After quizzing Adams, he decided to go upstairs and check on the couple. When he got to Miss Law's bedroom he saw her lying across the bed on her back with her legs dangling, her feet barely touching the floor, an image that would haunt him and change his life forever, an image that would render Cox, a gentle, sensitive man, incapable of working during the five years that followed. Miss Law had been stabbed to death. Perry was nowhere in sight.

Cox ran back downstairs and told Adams what he had found. He immediately called the Sevier County Sheriff but neither he nor Adams conducted any further search to find Perry. When Sheriff Whaley arrived a short time later with Bill Reagan, the Sevierville Chief of Police and Sevier County Coroner, they found Perry in the kitchen.

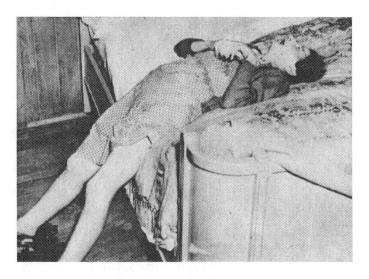

Josie Law as found in her bedroom

Perry was lying face down in a large pool of blood. He had been tortured, beaten, and stabbed. His feet had been burned with matches and cigarettes and spent matches were found in his shirt pocket. Perry had been bound in a chair as evidenced by burn marks on his wrists, but his hands were not bound when his body was found. There was a broken stool near the body that appeared to have been used to hit Perry. He had been stabbed in the jugular area of the neck and a woman's slip was wrapped around his neck. The slip would spawn two different theories. One was that the slip was used as a torture tool in choking Perry. The other was that Perry was not dead when the killers left and he retrieved it from a nearby clothes hamper in an effort to stop the bleeding. There were two butcher knives lying on the kitchen table but neither appeared to have been used.

Several hours later, after Perry's body had been removed and taken to Rawlings-Miller Funeral Home in Sevierville, the evidence of torture became more apparent. Because of the amount of blood on Perry's body, the severity of the rope burns on his wrists or the number of cuts on his body was not observed until his body was cleansed. A funeral home attendant counted 14 slashes about the face and neck and a number of bruises. His right hand was also bruised, indicating that he fought his attackers.

Chief and Coroner Reagan with Perry

Almost 60 years later one of the Rawlings-Miller Funeral Home attendants at Perry's Camp that day, Gene Catlett, recounted the slashes on Perry's face and neck. The slashes appeared to have been made by someone holding a pin knife between their thumb and index finger with the tip extending a quarter inch or so and then taking controlled swipes down the sides of his face and neck. The slashes were torture swipes. The fatal wound was a deep knife stab in his left lower neck. Catlett did not see Perry's entire body but knows that Perry's genitals were not removed, or even harmed, as was later rumored. He recalled that Perry's body was taken to Cleveland from Rawlings while Josie Law's body remained and laid in state at the funeral home one night before being taken to Blount County the following day. Catlett, in recalling the events surrounding the Perry murders, interjected that it was obvious to him and others who came in contact with Perry's relatives that they were only interested in Perry's estate and the money they stood to gain from its settlement.

Miss Law, like Perry, was fully clothed when found. Wearing a red-checked house dress, she had been stabbed twice in the left breast. Her glasses were partially off her face. In one of her hands, she clutched a finger end ripped from a red rubber glove. Miss Law had no other wounds and was believed to have died almost instantly. Chief Reagan estimated the time of both deaths between 10:00 and 11:00 p. m. the previous evening.

Very shortly after arriving at Perry's Camp, Sheriff Whaley had requested assistance from two other departments—the Tennessee Highway Patrol and the Knoxville Police Department. Others subsequently involved in the initial crime scene investigation included Highway Patrolman Robert Beadle, stationed in Gatlinburg, and Knoxville Police Department Detective Sergeant Archie Settlemire, Detective Henry Morris, and fingerprint experts E. A. Lloyd, A. R. Freeman, and Bill Beckler.

Mr. Beckler, who was 29 years of age at the time, was only one of two members of the joint law enforcement team that examined the initial crime scene found to still be alive. After 59 years he was unable to recall any specific, significant details in addition to those reported in the Knoxville newspapers. Mr. Beckler, who worked for the FBI before and after his stint with the Knoxville Police Department, still had a March 1950 issue of *Timely Detective*, a crime magazine, containing an account of the Perry Camp's murders. Mr. Beckler retired from the FBI's Knoxville Field Office with 30 years' service.

E. A. Lloyd, Chief Reagan, A. F. Freeman, William Beckler

No prints of value were found and no other physical evidence of possible significance was located. The river bank was searched in an effort to recover the knife used in the attacks since the murder weapon was not found at the murder scene. No money was found on the premises other than $28 in small change found concealed in a hotplate and a one dollar bill found near Perry's body. Perry had a safe but there was no indication it had been tampered with. Later, when it was opened, no money was found, only neatly stacked papers. A cigar box in which Perry was known to have kept money was missing as were a 45-caliber handgun and two black jacks. An exact figure as to the amount of money taken could not be determined, but the best estimate was later put at $7,000 to $8,000 by Cocke County Sheriff Charles Fisher.

As a result of Sheriff Whaley's requests for help and the subsequent searches that ensued, the bodies of Perry and Law remained at the crime scene until late afternoon. As a result, and as the word spread about the murders, more and more curiosity seekers came to Perry's Camp that afternoon. People lined up and toured the restaurant and kitchen, peering through the kitchen door at Perry's mutilated and tortured body still lying on the floor. It was estimated that literally hundreds of people showed up to view the scene and Perry's body before the authorities were finished and the day was done. The scene took on an atmosphere reminiscent of the exhibits area at a county fair.

Aside from the obvious physical evidence and the dusting for fingerprints, the law enforcement officers at the scene did not know of any other evidence of value to try to find. Technology had not yet been developed that would have prompted the officers to vacuum the crime scene for clues such as hairs and fibers and the like. There was no crime scene truck sitting out in the parking lot filled with technology and technicians capable of performing almost miraculous "CSI" type analyses. Neither was there a television news team on site recording every movement of the officers. Perhaps that's why so many gawkers showed up. That was the only way to get a look-see.

Jack Adams later told Sheriff Whaley that he had gotten off work at 10:00 p. m. the previous evening, had gone home, but had then gone for a ride with some friends and passed by Perry's Camp again 30 minutes later but saw nothing unusual. He passed by again between midnight and 12:30 a. m. when he noticed the neon sign was still on, which was unusual. He never observed any activity on either occasion.

Adams also told Sheriff Whaley, when asked if there had been anyone about whom Perry had expressed concern, that there had been a man in the restaurant 2-3 weeks before that Perry had pointed out to Miss Law. Perry was concerned because of the man's presence, and he indicated he feared this man. Adams did not know or hear this man's name but knew he would recognize him if he saw him again. Adams would later identify Claude Robertson as this man.

The immediate assumption, of course, was that robbery was the motive for the killings. There had always been the rumors about Perry hiding money on the premises. Chief Reagan estimated that Perry could have accumulated as much as $100,000 over the previous 20 years but doubted it was all hidden or buried at the tourist court. On the morning of the murders, Chief Reagan had met Perry on the sidewalk in Sevierville and had stopped and talked to him. Perry told him then he was on the way to the Bank of Sevierville.

In addition to the assumption that robbery was the motive, Sheriff Whaley had to surmise it was very likely Perry knew his attackers and that both Perry and Miss Law were killed to prevent identification.

The honeymoon couple determined by Jack Adams to have already gone when he arrived at work was identified as Mr. and Mrs. F. F. Ruckriegel of St. Matthews, Kentucky. The Ruckriegels had left early but returned later in the day after hearing a newscast about the murders. They had gone to bed early and left early without hearing any disturbance. Their cabin, located near a noisy spring, was some 75 yards from the restaurant.

The day following the discovery of the bodies at Perry's Camp, five well-known Knoxvillians went to the Knoxville Police Department to report they had run out of gas near Perry's Camp at about 11:30 p. m. on Monday evening and had gone into the tourist court office to make a phone call to someone in Gatlinburg or Sevierville for help. They entered the office when they found the front door unlocked. The neon sign was on but the inside of the building was dark. When no one came out they turned on the lights and found the wall telephone. They made their call for help and left a quarter on the telephone. While inside they heard a slight noise in the back but didn't think anything about it at the time. A car passed by out front very slowly twice while they were in the building. As they were leaving the area they observed a car bearing a Tennessee license plate with three occupants that turned toward Gatlinburg.

Based on the statements of these Knoxville motorists, it appeared very likely that the killers were still in the building when they arrived to call for help. Had they made more overt attempts to find someone inside the building, there could have very well have been seven homicides rather than two as the killers by then had possession of Perry's 45-caliber handgun.

Perry's Camp September 20, 1949

The man standing near the left edge of the above photograph wearing a hat is "Rel" Maples, owner of the Gatlinburg Inn, a charter member of the Gatlinburg Hotel-Motel Association which included tourist courts such as Perry's Camp, the first tourist court in the area. The tall, slender man standing next to Maples is Harold Atchley of Atchley's Funeral Home in Sevierville. Atchley in all probability knew Charlie Perry and Josie Law, but there was another reason he was present at Perry's Camp the day the bodies were found.

In those days the only ambulance service in Sevier County was offered by the two funeral homes—Rawlings-Miller and Atchley's. According to Gene Catlett the funeral homes would receive the call for emergency service at the same time but the first to respond to the scene got the business. On that day Rawlings-Miller got to Perry's Camp first. Catlett and another Rawlings-Miller attendant, Tom

Perry's Camp September 20, 1949

Harmon, were the first to arrive. He was familiar with Perry's Camp as he had gone there with his father when he was younger. He recalled that day was a non-funeral day,

and he and the other Rawlings-Miller attendants at the scene, were all wearing khaki slacks. This was the usual attire when the funeral home had no funeral scheduled for the day. Catlett recalled his being in the preceding photograph along with his co-workers on the front page of the Knoxville newspaper the following day.

Almost 60 years after the preceding photographs were taken at Perry's Camp, Brownlee Reagan, a 23-year-old Gatlinburg native and a Tennessee Highway Patrolman assigned at Lenoir City in September, 1949, would relate his recollections about the crime scene and the evening before the bodies were found. He had driven past Perry's Camp at about 10:00 P. M. the night before on his way home and recalled only that there were no inside lights on as he passed. He went to the crime scene the following day even though he was not assigned in Sevier County at the time. He knew both Charlie Perry and Josie Law. He could still recall Perry's body lying on the kitchen floor in his own blood with a cloth of some sort tied around his neck in tourniquet fashion indicating to him that Perry had done this himself in an effort to stop the bleeding from his neck wound.

Chapter 5

The Investigation and the Motives

This murder case, like all criminal cases, caused any number of theories and suspicions to spew forth. One of the first theories offered came from the Knoxville police chief who had been involved in solving the American Clothing theft 15 years previously. He suggested Perry's help in that matter might have caused a member of the Ernie Miller gang to finally seek revenge.

The day following the discovery of the murders at Perry's Camp, Knoxville detectives arrested Buford Roberts, an ex-convict and former member of the Miller gang, on a whiskey possession charge. Roberts, who had been released from prison during the summer, was one of those arrested in connection with the American Clothing case but was never convicted. Roberts was released the following day before the Knoxville chief had to answer a habeas corpus writ designed to free Roberts, which had been filed by Roberts' attorney. According to one of the Knoxville detectives assisting Sheriff Whaley in the Perry matter, Roberts had been taken to Sevier County for questioning but Whaley denied that story to the press. Roberts vanished without being charged with any crime in Sevier County.

Sheriff Whaley in the 2-3 days following the discovery of the bodies of Perry and Miss Law had been quoted as saying he had run into a "blank wall" in his investigation. On Friday of that week all that changed. He received information from Cocke County Sheriff Charles Fisher that a Robert Gunter, a convicted felon who had served time in the federal prison at Ashland, Kentucky with Sevier Countian Claude Robertson, had advised Sheriff Fisher that Robertson had come to him earlier in the week and asked him to hold some money for him. A portion of the money was in envelopes bearing "C. J. Perry." The total sum of the monies, which consisted of both coin and currency, was $975.35.

Sheriff Whaley was familiar with Robertson, the eldest son of former Sevier County Sheriff Marion Robertson. He knew that Robertson only lived about three miles from Perry's Camp and that he was a convicted felon, having served state time for voluntary manslaughter and federal time for forging a government check. He had only been released from federal prison less than two months before the Perry's Camp killings. Sheriff Whaley knew he was on the right track and immediately obtained an arrest warrant for Robertson. Robertson was located and arrested late that afternoon at the residence of Hattie Moore Greene, sister of Robertson's former wife, Reba, and Moses "Mosey" Moore in McMahon Addition, which at that time was locally known as "Frog Alley."

Robertson was sitting in a black 1940 Ford parked in front of the Greene house. Mosey Moore was talking to Robertson through the passenger side window. Robertson was arrested by Sheriff Whaley and either two or three Tennessee Highway Patrolmen—two of whom were believed to be Carson Webb and Robert Beadle. He was later transported to Newport where he was lodged in the Cocke County Jail.

According to Velda Greene Seagle, Hattie Greene's daughter, who was 10 years old at the time and witnessed Robertson's arrest, Sheriff Whaley had been at their house earlier in the day looking for Robertson. Her mother called the law when Robertson showed up at the house because he had been making it known that he was out kill her Uncle Mosey.

She never learned the reason for his making the threats toward her uncle, but does know that Robertson almost beat Mosey to death once while both were drunk together in Knoxville. Velda, a court reporter, recounted the events of that day years later with Brownlee Reagan, a Tennessee Highway Patrolman at the time, while she was employed by Sevierville Attorney Bob Ogle. Velda's recollection was that Brownlee was one of the arresting officers; however, Brownlee advised that was not the case. Brownlee was at that time living in Gatlinburg but working in Lenoir City. Velda further recalled that Claude had reportedly called attention to himself in the Perry case because he had been flashing $100 bills. She also recalled that her mother and her Aunt Ruth Moore Allen attended Claude Robertson's trial and that Ruth visited Robertson a number of times at the state penitentiary in Nashville.

Robertson, initially interviewed by Sheriffs Whaley and Fisher on Saturday morning, denied having given any money to Gunter and professed his innocence in the Perry's Camp murders. He insisted he had been with a woman from North Carolina, a Joyce Buchanan, age 35, at the Dixie Hotel in Johnson City the night of the murders.

Sheriffs Whaley and Fisher traveled to Johnson City following their interview of Robertson to interview Ms. Buchanan and to cover additional leads as developed. Ms. Buchanan had been located by the Johnson City police and placed in jail to await questioning by Sheriff Whaley. Ms. Buchanan related she had spent most of Tuesday with Robertson but failed to support his alibi that he had been with her the previous evening. She told them Robertson had traded an old Plymouth for a new Desoto at Johnson City. Ms. Buchanan was brought back to Cocke County Jail but was subsequently released from custody.

The trade of the old Plymouth (Hermie Lee Jones' car) for the new Desoto was reported in the September 26th issue of *The News-Sentinel*, Knoxville's evening newspaper at the time and was attributed to statements made by Ms. Buchanan to Johnson City police officers. In its issue two days earlier reporting the arrest of Robertson at Sevierville, *The News-Sentinel* reported Robertson was driving a 1940 model car and quoted Cocke County Sheriff Charles Fisher that the car had been purchased by Robertson that week. A cousin of Robertson, who was 14 years of age at the time and who closely followed the case, insisted the car which Robertson purchased that week and was in his possession when arrested, was a 1940 Ford 2-door sedan.

Joyce Buchanan

The information about the car was confirmed by Velda Seagle and by life-long Sevier County resident J. R. Layman. Layman in September, 1949 was a 22-year-old employee of Robertson Brothers Hardware on Court Avenue in Sevierville, two doors from the courthouse. Over 59 years later, J. R., a friend and patron of Charlie Perry and Josie Law, somewhat emotionally recalled Claude Robertson pulling into the lot of the hardware a couple of days after the bodies of Charlie and Josie had been found. Claude, whom J. R. had known for several years, was driving a 1940 Ford Deluxe 2-door sedan, solid black, which looked brand new. Layman took particular notice of the car, pointing out this 1940 Ford had two taillights rather the usual one taillight like most. Layman owned one of the one-taillight 1940 Fords. Robertson informed Layman he had bought the car at Newport.

Claude Robertson had come to Robertson Brothers Hardware that day to purchase a box of .38 caliber shells. One of the owners (and the author's uncle), Paul Robertson, refused to sell the ammunition to Claude, and he left empty-handed. Paul Robertson and Claude Robertson, like the author's mother, shared the same great-grandfather and were second cousins.

When they returned to Newport on Saturday evening, Sheriff Fisher had to respond to a shooting in the Bybee area of Cocke County. Sheriff Whaley resumed interview of Robertson upon his return to the jail. When confronted with the failure of Ms. Buchanan to provide him an alibi, Robertson admitted he had given the money to Gunter for him to hold and that he had been "at Perry's Camp when the money was got." He insisted he was the "lookout" during the robbery and identified Hermie Lee and Basil Jones, brothers from Fall Branch in Washington County, as his accomplices. Robertson told Sheriff Whaley they had taken two cars to the vicinity on that evening and left one parked about a mile away off the road toward Pigeon

Forge. The three of them drove to Perry's Camp in a Plymouth sedan. Robertson told Sheriff Whaley the three of them had been in the vicinity of Perry's Camp the night before (Sunday) to do the robbery but backed off after seeing a car parked there. Sheriff Fisher released information following interrogation of Robertson that between $7,000 and $8,000 was taken in the robbery.

On the next day (Sunday), which was the fifth day following discovery of the victims' bodies at Perry's Camp, Hermie Lee Jones was arrested as he was getting off from work at a fiber plant in Kingsport by Sheriff Whaley, THP Lieutenant Frank Williams, Washington County Sheriff Bob Hannabas, and two Kingsport police officers. Basil Jones was arrested while walking along a road in Fall Branch the same day by Sheriffs Whaley and Hannabas and Lt. Williams.

Sheriff Whaley, Hermie Lee Jones, Basil Jones, Sheriff Fisher, Claude Robertson

The Jones brothers were initially taken to the Washington County Jail in Jonesborough. When they first saw one another Hermie Lee yelled at Basil and told him "keep your damned mouth shut." That same evening both Jones were transported to and lodged in the Cocke County Jail in Newport. The only statement of any sort from the Jones came from Hermie Lee who acknowledged he had been in federal prison with Robertson at Ashland, Kentucky but that he had not seen Robertson since leaving prison.

The same day the Jones brothers were arrested, Sheriffs Whaley and Hannabas and Lt. Williams, with the consent of Mrs. Oma Jones, mother of Hermie Lee and Basil, and in her presence, searched the Jones home located near Fall Branch in Washington County. The only item seized as a result of the search was a 45-caliber pistol from which the serial number had been filed off. Two days later and eight days after the robbery and murders, Sheriff Whaley and other officers returned to the Jones property when no one was at home and searched the barn and the surrounding woodland.

Found under a bed of hay in the loft of the barn was a white pillow case stamped "Perry," containing a receipt of $35 to Charles Perry dated June 15, 1949 from Mrs. M. B. McMahan; a duplicate bank deposit crediting $203.07 to the account of C. J. Perry at the Bank of Sevierville dated June 14, 1949; an old-time $10 bill and a $1 bill of the same size; a key holder containing four keys; and a knotted small green cord. The barn had tobacco hanging in it when searched, and as a result it was dark and difficult to see in the loft. In order to locate the pillow case, the searching officers removed several boards from the barn's front along the roof line in order to get light into the loft, indicating that they knew exactly where to search. Also found on the property in the ashes of a fire were blood-stained charred scraps of clothing. Robertson had admitted he was present when this fire was burning.

A Robertson relative advised the most salvageable piece of clothing from the fire was a shirt collar bearing the laundry mark of one of Claude's sisters who had loaned him the shirt a few days before the murders. Claude had spent the night at her house after getting out of the Knox County jail on a charge of public drunkenness. This same relative advised that Sheriff Whaley was tipped by a waitress at a Sevierville restaurant about Claude spending money and saying things that made her suspicious enough to report it. According to this relative, when Sheriff Whaley talked to Claude after receiving this tip, Claude confessed and implicated the Jones brothers.

Jones Property in Washington County in September 1949

On Monday, September 26th, the arrests of Robertson and the Jones brothers became national news via the Associated Press. The article furnished details of the crime, identifying information of those being held, and quoted Sheriff Fisher as saying the three were being held in the Cocke County Jail for "safekeeping." This article was located in newspapers in Indiana, Pennsylvania; Anniston, Alabama; San Antonio, Texas; Billings, Montana, and others. *The Dothan Eagle* in Dothan, Alabama positioned it on the sports page between "public notices" and a story about Chicago mobster Frank Costello trying to take over the gambling rackets in Orlando. *The Herald Press*, St. Joseph, Michigan cornered the article on page 6 next to a photograph of U. S. Supreme Court Chief Justice Tom C. Clark sitting for a portrait wearing his robe with his familiar bow tie. The *Reno Evening Gazette* opted to sandwich the story between a photograph of Miss Europe and an instructional article on how to play canasta in the entertainment section, which carried primarily club ads including one for Harrah's and movies playing including "White Heat" with James Cagney.

From the outset, through the investigation and the trial, the motive for the murder of Charlie Perry and Josie Law, at least from what was made public, appeared to be robbery. Perry was tortured with cigarettes and matches, slashed with a knife, hit on the head with a wooden stool, and finally stabbed to death to make him divulge the location of cash at Perry's Camp. Josie Law had been stabbed twice through the heart to prevent her from ever identifying the attackers.

Josie Law knew her killer well. She had served beer to him when nobody else would. Charlie Perry had refused to serve Robertson on numerous occasions between his stints in prison and usually just told him to get out when Claude showed up at his place. But there was an additional motive behind the murder of Perry. There had been bad blood between Perry and Robertson for an unknown number of years, and unfortunately, for an unknown reason.

At some time between Robertson's arrest in July 1940 and his trial a year later for the murder of Bun Ward, Perry loaned the Wards $2,000 to go toward the prosecution of Robertson. The Wards are believed to have used the

46

money to hire George Shepherd as a private prosecutor. Perry suspected that Robertson burned down his power house following his release from prison in the Ward case in 1943. If this was true, this meant that Robertson had in all likelihood learned about the $2,000 loan. No corroboration of Perry's suspicion has become known.

In view of the bad blood that had existed for years between Robertson and Perry, it is very likely Robertson's motive in killing Perry was as much revenge, if not more so, than robbery. The robbery was a convenient fringe benefit, a payoff of an estimated $8,000 ($73,000 in 2008 dollars) that allowed him to relish the crime even more. By killing Perry, Robertson not only got revenge, he got a 1940 Ford.

Chapter 6

The Defendants

Claude Robertson

Claude Edgar Robertson, 40 years of age at the time of the Perry's Camp murders, was the first of ten children in his family. His father, Marion Robertson, a farmer, was elected to three 2-year terms as Sevier County Sheriff during the late 1920s and early 1930s. His father, a veteran of the Spanish American War, died in 1953 at age 74. Robertson's mother had died of paralysis (stroke) in 1945 at age 63. Only one of his siblings preceded him in death, a brother, Robert Marion, who died in France in August 1944 while serving in the U. S. Army.

Claude Robertson's generation was the last Robertson generation conceived to work the farm and live off the land in Sevier County. Like his father, his grandfather, and his great-grandfather before him, large families had been reared and had worked the fertile land in the Pigeon Forge, Red Bank, and Maples Branch areas of Sevier County since the early 19th Century. Their farms were in the rich river bottom lands along the West and Middle prongs of the Little Pigeon Rivers. Robertson's great-grandfather, Dio Cleason Robertson, who had come to Sevier County in about 1825 from South Carolina, came from a long line of farmers, Christians, and soldiers. The Robertsons matriculated from Virginia, to the Carolinas, then to Sevier County. They were devout Baptists, family men, and patriots. They acquired all the land they could to farm. They fought in the Revolutionary War, the Civil War, the Spanish American War, and both World Wars. This way of living had been the way of the Robertsons for generations and was the case with Claude Robertson's generation. Claude, however, was an exception.

Claude Robertson was a loner and, aside from crime and meanness, never really succeeded at anything. He grew up doing things that had to be red flags to everyone that knew him. He reportedly killed small animals growing up and later, when he had a disagreement with someone, he allegedly killed pets to satisfy his need for revenge. Growing up, and after he was grown, he was whipped by his father when he did something wrong or got into trouble. Claude never raised a hand to his father.

Robertson by all accounts seemed to enjoy being feared and having the reputation of someone who should be feared. During the 1940's there were teenage boys growing up in Sevierville who feared Robertson and were reluctant to even pass him on the same side of the street. One such teenager at that time talked about how he did cross the street once to avoid walking past Robertson. Robertson looked at him, smiled, and said, "You don't have to be afraid of me. I'm not going to hurt you." Robertson was a carouser, a heavy drinker, a gambler, and worst of all, a killer.

Newport, the county seat of Cocke County 25 miles away, afforded Robertson all the carousing, drinking, gambling, and whatever else he wanted. Newport in those days was very much like Phoenix City, Alabama—"wide-open," lawless, and corrupt. Robertson spent a lot of time in Newport. A frequent companion of Robertson when he went to Newport was Johnny Hicks, who was about the same age as Robertson and lived just off Newport Highway a few miles east of Sevierville. Once when they went to Newport together, and the last time for Hicks, Robertson got drunk and mad at Hicks. Robertson, who has been described as "the meanest drunk you'd ever want to meet," pulled a knife on Hicks and slashed his face and chest, creating scars that stayed with Hicks as reminders of Robertson the rest of his life. There was a crime waiting in Robertson's future that would bear the same earmarks as the assault on Hicks. Before the day of that crime arrived, however, Robertson would kill someone else.

On a July evening in 1940, Claude Robertson shot-gunned Pigeon Forge resident "Bun" Ward near Ward's residence on Possum Hollow Road (now Ridge Road) in Pigeon Forge following an afternoon argument over a poker game. A year later he was convicted of voluntary manslaughter and sentenced to eight years in prison. He was granted parole after serving 19 months at Brushy Mountain State Prison at Petros. He had satisfactorily completed his parole when he was arrested by the Knoxville Police Department on March 17, 1947 for felonious assault. This case was dismissed on May 6, 1947. (Information relative to this 1947 arrest was obtained from Robertson's Tennessee prison file which contains no further details. The victim of this assault is believed to have been Moses "Mosey" Moore, Robertson's alleged crime partner. The date of its occurrence and of its circumstances conforms with the information furnished by Harold V. Allen and Velda G. Seagle, first cousins whose uncle was Mosey Moore. Harold's recollection was that Mosey never reported the assault to police and called his own ambulance while Velda recalled Mosey went to a nearby house where police and an ambulance were summoned. Velda also recalled Robertson served no jail time for his assault of Mosey.

On May 28, 1947 Robertson pled guilty in federal court in Knoxville to an indictment charging him with forging and cashing a stolen U. S. Treasury check made out in the amount of $77.94 and received a 3-year sentence. A co-defendant in the case, Tim "Red" England, also of Sevier

County, pled guilty as well and received a 5-year sentence. Robertson was committed to the U. S. Penitentiary, Terre Haute, Indiana on May 29th but was transferred September 19th to the Federal Correctional Institute at Ashland, Kentucky where he served most of his federal time. Hermie Lee Jones and Robert Gunter were at Ashland during the same time period. Robertson was conditionally released on August 4, 1949—47 days before the tortured and stabbed bodies of Charles Perry and Josie Law would be found.

Robertson married once—on September 1, 1928. Robertson married Reba Moore, a younger sister of Mosey Moore, at Newport. The marriage bond reflects both of them added two years to their actual ages of 19 and 17. Claude and Reba lived in Pigeon Forge and Claude worked as a farmer. In about 1939 Reba left Claude, divorced him, and several years later married Herbert Martin, a sailor she met in New Orleans. Claude and Reba's union produced no children; however, they remained friends and maintained a close relationship for years following their separation and divorce.

Claude & Reba

51

In addition to farming on the family farm with his father, Robertson had also worked as a truck driver for the Sevier County Road Commission for eight years. For the first four months of 1947, prior to his federal sentence in the check case, he worked for Chess & Wymond, Inc., a wooden barrel stave company in Knoxville. Robertson had a third grade education and never served in the military service. He was classified 4F by the Selective Service Board.

During the four year period between 1943—after Robertson's parole in the Ward case—and 1947 when he went to federal prison—he would come into Perry's place from time to time for a beer but was seldom served. Perry would usually just tell him to leave which Claude, of course, did not like. Ev Whaley confirmed Perry's attitude toward Robertson in his conversation with Mack Marshall. And, according to the Ward descendants, one of Bun Ward's sisters worked for Perry and would not serve Robertson. Jo was the only one of the three that would serve him.

Perry's refusal to serve Robertson was also confirmed by Howard McMahan, a Sevierville taxi cab driver in 1949. McMahan took Robertson to Perry's Camp several times and "Perry put him out a time or two." McMahan hauled Robertson all over Sevier County but never outside the county. A frequent destination of Robertson was the Moore home in Frog Alley. McMahan never knew Robertson to own a car; he went everywhere by cab. The only car McMahan ever saw Robertson driving was a car owned by his brother, a school teacher (Tip Robertson). Robertson was always by himself. One of Robertson's associates, Johnny Hicks, never had a car, and he, like Robertson, traveled everywhere by cab. Hicks was also a frequent patron of Perry's Camp.

Another patron who knew Perry's Camp perhaps better than anyone still living was J. R. Layman, the hardware employee who later saw the 1940 Ford purchased by Robertson with proceeds from the robbery of Perry. J. R. was a frequent customer of Perry's and both admired and appreciated the way Perry conducted his business. According to Layman, Perry was a good businessman and Perry's Camp was always a pleasant and popular place to stop for a sandwich or a beer. Perry never allowed anyone to become unruly, annoying, or disruptive. If they did, he "put them out." He knew that Claude Robertson had been put out by Perry but was never present when this actually occurred.

Hermie Lee Jones

Hermie Lee Jones, age 26 when arrested at Kingsport on September 25th for robbery and murder in Sevier County, was single, working at Mead Corporation in Kingsport, and was living with his mother, Mrs. Oma Jones, and his 20-year-old brother, Basil, at Route 2, Fall Branch, Washington County. His father, Vannie Herbert Jones, had died in 1948 of asthma. His older brother, Haynes, also lived in Fall Branch and also worked at Mead Corporation.

At age 19, Hermie Lee had been drafted into the United States Army in March 1943 and was trained and assigned as a combat military policeman. In November, 1944 he was wounded in both legs while serving in France and was hospitalized in England for treatment and recuperation. Sometime between his hospitalization and January, 1946 Jones deserted the Army and after being apprehended, escaped.

After being taken into custody again he was court-martialed and sentenced to 20 years for Absent Without Leave (AWOL) and escape. On January 30, 1946 he was committed to the U. S. Penitentiary, Terre Haute, Indiana. On September 19, 1947 he was transferred to the Federal Correctional Institute at Ashland, Kentucky, after his sentence was commuted to six years. He was paroled

December 30, 1947 and was on parole when arrested on the Sevier County charges. Jones and Claude Robertson had been at Terre Haute at the same time and were transferred to Ashland on the same date. Hermie Lee, who had completed three years of high school but never graduated, received a dishonorable discharge from the U. S. Army.

Basil Buford Jones

Basil Jones, age 20 when arrested, was unemployed and living with his mother and his brother, Hermie Lee, at Fall Branch. He had never been in any trouble prior to September 25, 1949 when he was arrested while walking along a road in Fall Branch.

Basil, after completing two years of high school, had enlisted in the military service but the dates of service could not be confirmed. He served as a Private in the U. S. Army Air Force during 1946 and during its transition to the U. S. Air Force during 1947.

Basil was known to have been in the military in January, 1947 but was no longer in service when he had a near-death experience in May, 1948. A month before his 19th birthday he escaped virtually unscathed in a car wreck a few miles from his home when the car he was driving plunged off a 30-foot-high cliff flipping over six times. His 18-year-old passenger was thrown from the vehicle but also escaped with only scratches.

Chapter 7

The Prior Conviction of Robertson in "Bun" Ward's Killing

On Sunday afternoon, July 21, 1940 Claude Robertson showed up at the residence of Jim Vance on Possum Hollow Road (Ridge Road) in Pigeon Forge where four or five men, including Vance and Luther William "Bun" Ward, were playing poker. Robertson asked to join the game and the other players reluctantly agreed. Bun subsequently accused Claude of cheating, called him on it, and embarrassed him. The cheating incident was allegedly over a nickel. According to a Robertson descendant, Robertson and Ward got into a tussle and Ward was alleged to have struck Robertson with a pump handle. Robertson left, went home and got a shotgun, and then returned to the vicinity of Bun Ward's house, located on Possum Hollow Road a half mile or so from the card game. Robertson lay in the brush along Possum Hollow Road until Bun Ward approached walking home and then shot him once with the shotgun.

The account of the shooting in *The Knoxville Journal* reported that Ward was shot in the chest while *The Montgomery Vindicator* reported in its July 24th issue that Ward was shot under the arm and through the heart. The death certificate, signed by Dr. C. P. Wilson of Sevierville, Director of the Sevier County Public Health Department at the time, reflected the cause of death as a gunshot wound of the left subclavical artery. Neighbors heard the shot and found Ward dying in the road at about nine o'clock that night. Sheriff Ernest R. Conner told *The Journal* a warrant had been issued for Robertson for murder and *The Vindicator* reported that Robertson surrendered himself the following morning at his home to Sheriff Conner after getting medical attention for an undisclosed malady. *The Journal* also reported that Robertson's father had retained attorneys E. M. Creswell, T. C. Paine, and O. M. Connatser before surrendering his son to Sheriff Conner and that Robertson had spent the night at the home of his mother-in-law, Mrs. W. M. Moore (who lived on McMahan Avenue in Sevierville's McMahan Addition). *The Vindicator* also reported Robertson's father, F. M. Robertson, and J. Mack Sims had gone to the Ward home to warn them that Claude had come home and got a shotgun that afternoon following an argument with Ward, which report was retracted in the next week's issue as an error.

The same Robertson descendant who advised of the pump handle related that Robertson did go home but that his father, mother, and a sister, who were at home, were unable to stop him from leaving the house with a shotgun. The Robertson home place was located near what is now the intersection of Middle Creek Road and Teaster Lane, not far from Ridge Road. His father owned a house located along the way to the Ward residence that was occupied by another of Claude's sisters and her husband. Claude stopped there briefly then continued on to the Ward house where he shot and killed Bun Ward. According to this Robertson relative, Bun did have a knife in his hand. The Robertson family members who were at home heard the gunshot. This same relative also said, however, that Claude's former wife, Reba, lied for him at his trial about his having the shotgun to give to her brother to go hunting.

At the time of his death, Bun Ward was 32, worked part time for the State Highway Department and also farmed. He was a member of a large, well-known Pigeon Forge family that included six brothers and five sisters. His father was a Southern Railway engineer.

Robertson appeared before County Judge James C. Allen (the author's uncle) the following Friday and waived a preliminary hearing. His bond was set at $7,500. The Assistant Attorney General handling the bond hearing was George G. Allen (the author's cousin). The case was not indicted until March, 1941 and did not come to trial until the July 1941 term of Sevier County Circuit Court. Robertson's attorneys included E. M. Creswell, a former attorney general, T. C. Paine, and O. M. Connatser. Joseph W. Wolfenbarger, a native of Grainger County, was the Attorney General and prosecutor of record, and the presiding judge was the Honorable W. D. McSween, a native of Newport. Judge McSween was not an elected Circuit Court Judge but rather had been appointed on an interim basis for the ailing circuit judge, W. P. (Pres) Monroe from Union County. Four months following the trial, George R. Shepherd, also of Newport and who also had filled in for Judge Monroe, was elected Judge of the Second Judicial Circuit.

The Sevier County jurors who decided the Ward case were as follows: W. M. Hart, T. W. Williams, Nelson Breeden, Hobart Walker, Newt Howard, Gene Rolen, Johnnie Barnes, B. A. Valentine, B. C. Dixon, Jimmie McCarter, Beecher Baxter, and Claude Rolen.

On July 11th, only ten days short of the anniversary date of the murder, Robertson was found guilty of voluntary manslaughter. Robertson's attorneys immediately filed a motion for a new trial which Judge McSween denied four days later. His attorneys then filed notice of appeal to the Supreme Court of Tennessee sitting in Knoxville but withdrew the appeal two days later, thus accepting the verdict and sentence handed down by the jury.

Robertson's motion for a new trial filed by his attorneys had been based on Judge McSween's denying testimony from two witnesses, Ray Ward (no relation to the victim) and Gordon Parrott, whose testimony, according to the defense, would have supported that of Robertson, who had taken the stand in his own defense. Robertson had testified that Ward and Parrott had taken him home from the poker game and had agreed to wait for him or to come back to his house to pick him up and take him to Sevierville. He had needed a ride to Sevierville to meet his former wife and her brother who were coming to Sevierville from Kentucky. His former wife had asked Robertson in a letter, which he produced as evidence, to bring one or more shotguns with him, that her brother wanted to go squirrel hunting the following day.

When Ward and Parrott neither waited nor returned to pick him up, he started walking to Sevierville on his own and en route met Ward walking on the road. According to Robertson Ward approached him with an automobile pump in his right hand and a knife in his left hand and attempted to assault him. It was at this point, according to Robertson, that he shot Ward in self-defense with the shotgun he was taking to his former brother-in-law in Sevierville. Robertson testified that Ward, not he, was the aggressor. Judge McSween ruled that Ward and Parrott could testify only that they took Robertson home, and that they neither waited nor came back for him, but could testify to nothing beyond that. They would not have been permitted to testify to any arrangements that had allegedly been made to take Robertson to Sevierville. Robertson's attorneys argued that exclusion of this testimony denied Robertson his right to a defense of self-defense. Robertson's attorneys lost their argument, however, as Judge McSween overruled their motion for a new trial.

The Wards and their descendants have always contended that Robertson's father paid money to insure a conviction of a lesser charge and to insure a light sentence. In Mack Marshall's June 1990 interview of Ev Whaley, Ev told Marshall … "Claude shot old Bun Ward down with a shotgun, and Charlie loaned them Ward's … two thousand dollars to prosecute Claude, and that's what it all started over—between 'em … Between the murder case and so forth … because when Claude got out of the penitentiary, I was still working for Charlie, and he says—I said Charlie how come your power house burned down? He said, 'Well Ev, I don't want you to mention it, but Claude Robertson's out of the pen now, and something could have happened worse than that, you see.'" A Ward descendant confirmed that Perry gave or loaned $2,000 to Jim Ward, Bun's brother, to help with the prosecution of Robertson. Jim and Bun Ward were described as being "joined at the hip," meaning, of course, they were very close. The Ward descendants most familiar with this do not know what was done with the money.

Luther "Bun" Ward

Gene Catlett, the Rawlings-Miller Funeral Home attendant who was among the first to respond to Perry's Camp when the bodies were found, unknowingly provided an explanation about the use of the $2,000. He recalled that the Ward family hired George Shepherd, who later became a Circuit Court judge, to prosecute Claude Robertson for "Bun" Ward's murder. Catlett, although only 11 years old at the time, has a vivid memory of having attended the trial with his father and hearing testimony about the murder. He also recalled seeing another trial not too long after the Robertson trial in which George Shepherd, rather than being a prosecuting attorney, was the presiding judge.

The contention of the Ward descendants that someone in this case was paid off would have been a more viable allegation if aimed at a juror or jurors as opposed to the presiding judge. Robertson was charged with murder and the jury could decide if he was guilty or not guilty of first degree murder, second degree murder, or manslaughter, voluntary or involuntary. Efforts were made to determine if any of the jurors had any direct connection with Robertson or members of his family and nothing was found. The only connection between any member of this jury and the defendant pertained to one of his attorneys and not the defendant. A member of the jury did have a brother named after the father of one of Robertson's attorneys but no blood relation was ascertained. Otherwise, no connection of any kind was unearthed. Judge McSween presided in the case as an interim judge for an ailing Judge Monroe, and there was nothing found to suggest that he or anyone else involved in the case did anything unethical or illegal.

Epilogue

Almost two years before the future Sevier County Attorney General of 32 years, Alfred C. Schmutzer, Jr. was born, Claude Robertson stashed the shotgun he used to murder "Bun" Ward in a well shared by one of two rental houses which Schmutzer inherited from his mother. The house was located on Possum Hollow Road (Ridge Road) in Sevierville's Runyon Addition, three miles from the Ward house and murder scene. The house was rented by James R. Moore, Sr., the former brother-in-law of Robertson. This previously unknown fact came to light as a result of information shared by James R. Moore, Jr., who, although only two years of age in 1940, learned of this from family members. The location and description of the house was corroborated through Sevier County tax records, a 72-year-old life-time Runyon Addition resident, and Schmutzer.

In a twisted sort of way, this information was corroborated in another way by Robertson himself during his testimony at his trial in July, 1941. Robertson testified that he had received a letter from his former wife, Reba, who was at the time living in Kentucky, asking him to bring one or two shotguns to Sevierville on July 21, 1940 (the date of the murder), the date of her planned arrival. The letter, introduced as evidence at the trial, further stated that a brother, who was coming with her, wanted to borrow the shotgun(s) to go squirrel hunting. (A Robertson descendent disputed this story, saying that Reba lied for Claude in his defense.) Robertson appeared to have concocted a defense that had been woven around what are now known to have been partial truths.

Almost 69 years after Robertson discarded the murder weapon in the Runyon Addition well, an effort was made by former Attorney General Schmutzer, Steve O. Watson, and the author to recover the shotgun, and that effort was, unfortunately, unproductive. The well casing, which was large enough to allow the passage of a shotgun, was encased in an eight inch slab of concrete which also contained a drain bowl formed in the concrete. A long-handled pump was known to have been still in the casing during the 1940's but had long since been removed. The casing had filled with mud, sludge, and debris over a period of 50-60 years, making the well inaccessible. The shotgun hidden there by Robertson all those years before was there to stay. Even the most practical of efforts to retrieve the shotgun from its grave would have been cost prohibitive. Claude Robertson did not mean for the shotgun to be found, and it never will be.

Following is a photograph of the well casing and drain bowl taken on May 20, 2009. The knob end of a six foot iron pry bar inserted in the well casing some five feet can be seen sticking out a little over a foot. This was as far as the bar penetrated before hitting solid debris.

Ditched Shotgun Site

In addition to being only three miles from the Ward murder scene, this house and well were along the most logical route (formerly Possum Hollow Road, now Ridge Road) to the W. M. Moore home in McMahan Addition a little over a mile away where Robertson spent the night before turning himself in the following morning at his father's house in Pigeon Forge.

Chapter 8

The Trial

Sevier County Courthouse 2008

The Sevier County Courthouse was, of course, the site of all court proceedings. The courthouse, completed in 1895, underwent major renovations during the early 1970's. The front landing, encased in a stone wall with steps at both ends, did not exist in 1949. Instead, the extra wide front steps simply cascaded down from the wide double doors entrance.

On September 30, 1949, ten days following the murder of Perry and Ms. Law, the three defendants were indicted for the murder of Perry. The 2-page indictment in its entirety follows.

I N D I C T M E N T

THE STATE   )
)   No. 1132
VS.   )
)   INDICTMENT - MURDER
CLAUDE ROBERTSON, ALIAS,   )
HERMIE LEE JONES, ALIAS,   )   J. Roy Whaley, Prosecutor
BASIL B. JONES, ALIAS   )

STATE OF TENNESSEE, COUNTY OF SEVIER

CIRCUIT COURT FOR SEVIER COUNTY JULY TERM, 1949

      The Grand Jurors for the State of Tennessee, having been
duly summoned, elected, impanelled, sworn and charged to inquire
for the body of the county of Sevier and State aforesaid, upon
their oath aforesaid, present, that Claude Robertson, Alias,
Hermie Lee Jones, Alias, and Basil B. Jones, Alias, on the --
day of September, 1949, in the State and County aforesaid, did
unlawfully, feloniously, wilfully, deliberately, premeditatedly,
maliciously and with malice aforethought make an assault upon the
body of one Charlie Perry by cutting an stabbing and killing him,
the said Charlie Perry with certain deadly weapons, to-wit:
knives, and some other sharp instruments to the Grand Jurors,
unknown they the said Claude Robertson, Alias, Hermie Lee Jones,
Alias, and Basil B. Jones, Alias, then and there did unlawfully,
feloniously, wilfully, deliberatedly, premeditatedly, and of their
malice aforethought, kill and murder the said Charlie Perry contrary
to the statue, and against the peace and dignity of the State of
Tennessee.

                  Joseph W. Wolfenbarger, Attorney General

No. 1132 - INDICTMENT - THE STATE VS. CLAUDE ROBERTSON, ALIAS, ET
AL. - MURDER - J. Roy Whaley, Prosecutor.

      Witnesses: C. D. Fisher, Tom Harmon, Anna Mae Maples,
Bill Reagan, Blain Kelly, Robert Gunter, Robert Hanabas.

O O O O O 1 O 0 0 1 4

Clerk: Summon above named witnesses for the State.

               Jos. W. Wolfenbarger, Attorney General

     Witnesses sworn by me in the presence of the Grand Jury September 30, 1949.

     A. B. Shields, Foreman of the Grand Jury.

A TRUE BILL - A. B. Shields, Foreman of the Grand Jury; Freeman Ogle, W.H. Ownby, Joe Lane, Dewey Cook, Eliga Helton, Dewey Williamson, Frank Clabo, I. A. Henderson, W. H. Wayland, Thad Whaley, A. V. King, Roy Graves.

     Filed 30 day of September ,1949. H. T. Ogle, Clerk.

STATE OF TENNESSEE   )
) ss
COUNTY OF SEVIER   )

     I, H. T. Ogle, Circuit Court Clerk for Sevier County, Tennessee, hereby certify that the foregoing is a true, perfect, and correct copy of the Indictment, Judgment of Conviction and Mittimus, in the case of:

         STATE OF TENNESSEE VS. CLAUDE ROBERTSON, ALIAS,
                       HERMIE LEE JONES, ALIAS, No. 1132,

as the same appears of record and on file in my office in Criminal Minutes "C", page 493, in my office at Sevierville, Tennessee.

     Given under my hand and seal at office in Sevierville, Tennessee, this the 17th day of November, 1949.

                       H. T. Ogle

                       H. T. Ogle, Circuit Court
                       Clerk for Sevier County,
                       Tennessee

At the time of the indictment, the Honorable George R. Shepherd, the presiding Circuit Court judge, had promised the trial of Robertson and the Jones would begin on November 14th, and he kept his promise. Or at least as best he could.

Judge George R. Shepherd

Judge Shepherd of Newport was a seasoned, experienced judge who had already served eight years on the bench as the Judge of the Second Judicial District which included Sevier, Cocke, Union, Hancock, Grainger, and Jefferson Counties. He had a month before won the Republican primary in his bid for another term. He had been unopposed. Judge Shepherd was a veteran and was very active in the American Legion and veterans affairs.

A total of 400 prospective jurors were summoned, and of these, 15 failed to appear. In their cases, Judge Shepherd ordered that they pay fines of $25 and to show cause why they should not be jailed. Attorney General Joe W. Wolfenbarger had indicated his intention to seek the death penalty upon convictions, and having done so, was obligated to ask each prospective juror if he objected to "infliction of the death penalty if the law and the evidence warrant it." At the end of the first day six jurors had been selected out of 83 examined. Juror after juror was excused after advising he had formed an opinion about the case.

Beginning with day one and continuing on every day court was in session, there was an overflow crowd at the courthouse for the trial. The courtroom, a rather small courtroom on the top floor, was jam-packed and people were everywhere—in the halls, any empty rooms that could be found, outside on the steps and on the courthouse lawn. The courtroom regulars and local attaches believed the crowd to be the largest for a trial since the White Cap trial over 50 years before.

The preceding photograph, captioned "Spectators Fill Sevier Court House" appeared on the front page of the November 15, 1949 edition of *The News-Sentinel*. The text that accompanied the picture was "CAME TO SEE TRIAL-- The throng of spectators, above, on hand for the opening of the trial of three men accused in the slaying of a Gatlinburg tourist camp operator, Charles Perry, 70, and his 43-year-old housekeeper, Josie Law, is believed to be the largest for any trial held at Sevierville since the turn of the century."

Day two was less successful in selecting a jury than day one had been. With the entire day devoted to examining 163 potential jurors, only three were seated and added to the six chosen the day before. Many prospective jurors said they could not weigh the evidence impartially, that they had already formed an opinion about the case. Judge Shepherd remarked, "I have never worked as hard to get a fair and impartial jury. There's something wrong about this. Somebody's talking." Judge Shepherd continued by saying, "This is a dangerous situation when all these men say they can't listen to state evidence and listen to the defense and render an impartial verdict." When one juror remarked that he didn't think he could do what he thought was right, Judge Shepherd fired back, "It's not right to try to get off juries."

As the day dragged on Attorney General Wolfenbarger inadvertently failed to ask the stock question, "If the law and evidence warrants, have you any religious or conscientious scruples about inflicting the death penalty?" After the state had accepted one juror, he volunteered that he did not believe in capital punishment and would not vote to send any man to the electric chair. Judge Shepherd ruled the juror incompetent and defense attorneys Ray and Erby

Jenkins jumped to their feet with objections, claiming the juror had been selected by the state and could not now be rejected. The judge overruled their objection, and the defense filed an exception.

Attorney General Joseph W. Wolfenbarger, Sr. at Far Left

Attorney General Wolfenbarger, who had been at his job as the district's prosecutor since 1934, was accustomed to the long, tedious, and sometimes time-consuming process of quizzing prospective jurors. In February, 1936, at the beginning of the trial of three defendants for the murder of Union County Sheriff L. B. Hutcheson on December 6, 1935, there were 321 prospective jurymen called from a panel of 600 before a jury was seated. He was also experienced in seeking the death penalty as he had in the Hutcheson killing in which all three were sentenced to death by electrocution. The sentences for two of the defendants were commuted by newly-elected Governor Gordon

Browning in March, 1937; however, the sentence of the alleged shooter, Gus McCoig, was carried out on the morning of April 8th at the Nashville penitentiary.

The preceding photograph of Wolfenbarger standing around the pot-bellied stove with three other men was taken during the McCoig trial at the Union County Courthouse. The other men depicted in the photograph are, from left to right, Fred Myers, a criminal investigator; an unidentified agent of the Tennessee Bureau of Alcohol and Tobacco; and "Dutch" Swan, the Assistant Attorney General at that time who later became Attorney General. Wolfenbarger, who was 43 in this photograph, was 61 years old when the Perry murder case came to trial in Sevierville in November, 1949. He had the reputation of being a very competent trial lawyer and an aggressive Attorney General. He was re-elected and held the office for another nine years following the Perry case, thus serving as Attorney General for a total of 24 years. Wolfenbarger had been a practicing attorney for almost 60 years when he died in 1976 at age 82. The opposing counsel in this case was also impeccably qualified to try the case.

Hermie Lee and Basil Jones were represented by Ray and Erby Jenkins, partners in the same Knoxville law firm but no blood relation, along with Sevierville attorney O. M. Connatser. Robertson was represented by Sevierville attorney Clyde Bogart. Ray Jenkins, who had been practicing law for 30 years, was regarded by many as the best criminal defense attorney in East Tennessee. During the course of his long and distinguished career he would represent some 600 murderers. Five years following his appearance in this case, Jenkins was appointed chief counsel for the U. S. Senate committee investigating the Army-McCarthy hearings. Five years following his death in 1980 The Ray H. Jenkins Competition was founded by the Moot Court Board at the University of Tennessee where Jenkins graduated cum laude in 1920 after having passed the bar and getting his law license the year before.

Clyde Bogart, Erby Jenkins, Ray Jenkins, and O. M. Connatser

At the end of day two there were nine jurors seated. Judge Shepherd dismissed the remaining 139 members of the original 400-member panel and summoned a new panel of 150 new potential jurors.

By noon on day three a jury had finally been seated. The jury consisted of twelve white men between the ages of 35 and 60.

By this time literally hundreds of spectators had been in the courtroom, the halls, other rooms, and outside and the numbers never diminished. Spectators were bringing their lunches and eating in the courtroom. To leave would mean they would not get their seat back until the next day. Courtroom seats were being sold for two dollars. Again, this scene was much like the crime scene had been, reminiscent of a county fair and having a carnival-like atmosphere. Aside from the court officers the only people who had reserved seats in the courtroom were the relatives of Perry and Ms. Law. Their seats were near the judge's bench.

Following the lunch recess on day three, Sheriff Whaley would finally take the stand as the state's first witness. His testimony would center on the statements made by Robertson and Hermie Lee Jones, the circumstances surrounding the searches of the Jones property in Washington County on September 25th and 27th, and the items seized during the course of those searches. Sheriff Whaley would also lay the groundwork for the testimony of witnesses to follow.

Prior to Whaley's testimony beginning two of the jurors would make unsolicited comments to the court. One of the jurors, Sam Headrick, said, "I don't believe in capital punishment." The other, Burl Adams, said he would render a fair and impartial verdict "up to" capital punishment. Judge Shepherd cut short these statements, saying, "Too many jurors are saying things they are not asked about."

The first hour or more of Sheriff Whaley's testimony was outside the jury as it involved the admissibility of physical evidence he had seized following searches of the Jones property on two different days a week or so following the murders. Sheriff Whaley testified he located a 45-caliber pistol with the serial number filed off in an upstairs room of the Jones home after being granted consent to search the house by Mrs. Oma Jones. He pointed out a dent on top of the barrel.

Sheriff Whaley testified Mrs. Jones "said we could search any time." He went to the Jones home after having arrested the Jones brothers a few hours earlier. When they (Whaley, Hannabas, and Williams) arrived, no one was home. Sheriff Hannabas left and after a little while returned with Mrs. Jones. Sheriff Hannabas unlocked the door with Mrs. Jones standing behind him.

When Attorney General Wolfenbarger asked Whaley what he found in the house Ray Jenkins had objected, asking Whaley if he had a search warrant. Wolfenbarger argued the evidence should be let in with the jury out of the room but Jenkins had objected again. After this initial testimony, Hermie Lee Jones stood up at the defense table and shouted a taunt to the sheriff, "You wouldn't lie would you?"

Sheriff Whaley then testified about returning to the Jones property two days later and searching the barn and surrounding woodlands without a search warrant. He related having found the pillow case in the barn and testified as to each item found in the pillow case—the receipt, the deposit slip, the old money, the key holder, and the knotted small green cord. Concerning the keys found, Whaley testified he had directed Chief Reagan to fit these keys to Perry's car. Concerning the cord, he testified it compared "very close" in size to the burns found on the wrists of Perry after the body was discovered. Sheriff Whaley also testified that he found remains of a fire where clothing had been burned on the Jones property and that Robertson had admitted being present when the fire was burning.

Following arguments from both sides, with both sides citing case law to support their position, Judge Shepherd ruled Sheriff Whaley's searches valid and the evidence seized admissible.

During the remainder of day three and the morning of day four, Sheriff Whaley continued his testimony before the jury. He again testified about the searches and what he had found. Judge Shepherd allowed the items entered into evidence. He also testified as to statements made to him by Claude Robertson and Hermie Lee Jones. Robertson admitted traveling from Washington County to Newport in a taxi cab driven by James Ledford, a Johnson City taxi driver. Whaley testified Robertson admitted having given the $975.35 to Robert Gunter at Newport, that he was at Perry's

Camp when the money was stolen, and that he had served as a lookout for the robbery. Robertson further told him that he and two others had gone to Perry's Camp in two cars, but parked one a mile or so away, then rode in together in a Plymouth sedan. Sheriff Whaley also testified Robertson told him that they had originally planned to rob Perry the night before but backed off after seeing a car parked there.

Whaley testified that when the Jones brothers first saw each other at the Washington County jail after their arrests, Hermie Lee warned his brother to "keep your damned mouth shut." At this point the Jones brothers rose from their seats and Hermie Lee shouted, "You wouldn't lie, would you, Fisher?" Hermie Lee apparently had confused Whaley with Cocke County Sheriff Charles Fisher. Judge Shepherd rapped for order and told the Jones, "I can't put you in jail; you're already there." Sheriff Whaley's only other testimony about any statements made by Hermie Lee Jones was that he knew Robertson at the federal prison at Ashland, Kentucky, but had not seen Robertson since he (Jones) left Ashland.

In addition to the evidence found on the Jones property, the broken stool found next to Perry's body was entered into evidence. Sheriff Whaley also testified as to the wounds of Perry and Miss Law.

When Sheriff Whaley concluded his testimony and all the physical evidence was admitted just before the lunch break on day four, it became obvious to all that the defendants and their attorneys were concerned. Whaley's testimony and the physical evidence had landed an excruciating blow.

Immediately following the lunch recess Ray Jenkins held a whispered conference with Attorney General Wolfenbarger who then called a quick conference with other members of the prosecution outside the courtroom. Shortly thereafter the victims' relatives were asked to join the conference; it appeared to all that some sort of deal was in the works. After Jenkins received a message from the prosecution huddle, Robertson and the Jones brothers left the courtroom for a conference with their attorneys. When the groups came back into the courtroom, it was obvious to everyone that it was over. Sheriff Whaley had come back into the courtroom wearing a broad smile.

Robertson sat with the same stolid expression that he had shown throughout the proceedings. Hermie Lee and Basil Jones, however, were pale and red-eyed. They sat with their arms locked about each other. Then came the announcement that Robertson and Hermie Lee Jones would pled guilty to both the murder of Perry and Ms. Law and would be sentenced to 99 years in each case with the sentences to run concurrently. The judge and Wolfenbarger emphasized that under the sentencing agreement, both men would serve the entire time or until their death. Wolfenbarger told the jury it was unlikely that a stiffer sentence, which could only have been death in the electric chair, could have been achieved had the case been tried since there were men on the jury who could not vote for capital punishment.

The only evidence offered after the agreement was announced was a photograph of Ms. Law shortly after her body was discovered. Sheriff Whaley identified the photograph. This was the only evidence heard about her murder other than Sheriff Whaley's earlier testimony about her having been stabbed to death.

In pronouncing sentence, Judge Shepherd declared, "If anybody ought to go to the electric chair, you ought. This has been the most dastardly crime committed in this county since 1900." He also told the two that he would send with them "a statement that you two men should never be turned out of prison. You are dangerous."

Additionally, per the agreement a verdict of not guilty was entered as to Basil Jones and he was released from custody.

Sentiment against Robertson and Hermie Lee Jones was running so high that THP transported the two from the Sevier County Courthouse directly to the Brushy Mountain State Prison at Petros. The THP officials did not allow any pictures to be taken by the newspapers before leaving. The hasty departure was carried out to avert any possible acts of violence against the two.

This case was over much more quickly than it started. The state's case had hinged on the admissibility of the physical evidence found by Sheriff Whaley and other officers on the Jones property. Once Judge Shepherd had ruled in the state's favor, the case was pretty much over.

The following three pages reflect the actual changes of pleas, the verdict, and the sentences imposed.

STATE OF TENNESSEE   X

     VS   X   No. 1132 - MURDER

CLAUDE ROBERTSON, ALIAS,
HERMIE LEE JONES, ALIAS,
BASIL B. JONES, ALIAS,   X

    Came the Attorney General for the State of Tennessee with associate counsel and the defendants in person and by counsel and for plea to the charge says that they are not guilty and put themselves upon their country for their trial, and the Attorney General with associate counsel doth the like.

    Whereupon, came a jury of good and lawful men, citizens, freeholders or householders of Sevier County, Tennessee, to-wit: Jim Parton, J. R. Pitner, Elmer Huskey, Roy Huff, Horace Etherton, Oscar Riley, Jack Hodges, Bruce Moore, Rellie Whaley, Ashley Stinnett, Burl Adams and Sam Headrick, who were elected, empannelled and sworn to well and truly try the issues joined, wherein the State of Tennessee is plaintiff, and Claude Robertson, alias, Hermie Lee Jones, alias, and Basil B. Jones are defendants, and a true verdict render according to the law and evidence.

    After hearing a portion of the State's evidence two of the defendants, namely: Claude Robertson, alias and Hermie Lee Jones, alias, changed their pleas of not guilty and entered pleas of guilty of murder in the first degree.

    Whereupon, the jury was sworn to ascertain and fix the punishment wherein the State of Tennessee is plaintiff and Claude Robertson, alias and Hermie Lee Jones, alias, are defendants, according to the best of their skill and ability, do now report and say that they fix the defendants' sentences at ninety-nine years each in the State penitentiary for their said offense, of murder in the first degree.

It is therefore ordered by the Court that in accordance
with the finding of the Jury that the defendants undergo
confinement in the State Penitentiary for a period of Ninety-nine
years for the offense of murder in the first degree as fixed by
the jury at hard labor according to the rules and regulations
of that institution. Sentence imposed in this cause will run
concurrently with sentence imposed in case No. 1133.
The defendants will pay all costs that accrued in this
case for which execution may issue.

Upon recommendation of the attorney general for the State
with associate counsel that a verdict of not guilty be entered
in this cause as to Basil B. Jones, Alias. It is therefore
ordered by the Court that a verdict of Not Guilty be entered in
this cause as to the defendant Basil B. Jones, Alias, and that
the defendant be released from custody and for nothing held.

VERDICT AND SENTENCE

STATE OF TENNESSEE,   **Sevier**   COUNTY

Be it Remembered, That at a regular term of the Circuit Court of   **Sevier**   County, for the said County and State, begun and held in the Courthouse in the town of **Sevierville, Tennessee,** on the ....7th.... day of ..**November**......, 19.**49**, the same being the ....**First**.. Monday in **November**...... 19.**49**, present and presiding the Hon. ....**Geo. R. Shephard**........................., Judge, the following is of record:

STATE OF TENNESSEE   Indictment for .....**Murder**.....................

No. .**1132**   vs.

Claude Robertson, Alias,
Hermie Lee Jones, Alias,

Comes the Attorney-general on the part of the State, and the Defendant in proper person, who, being arraigned at the bar of the Court, and charged on the bill of indictment, pleads not guilty to the same, and for his trial puts himself upon the country, and the Attorney-general doth the like, when to try **Claude Robertson, Alias, Hermie Lee Jones, Alias,**

there came a jury of good and lawful men, to-wit:. **Jim Parton, J. R. Pitner,** **Elmer Huskey, Roy Huff, Horace Etherton, Oscar Riley, Jack Hodges,** **Bruce Moore, Rellie Whaley, Ashley Stinnett, Earl Adams, Sam Headrick,**

who, having been elected, tried, and sworn well and truly to try **the issues joined between** **the State of Tennessee, plaintiff, and Claude Robertson, Alias, and Hermie** **Lee Jones, Alias, Defendants**......, a true deliverance make and a true verdict render according to the law and evidence, who, upon their oath, do say that the Defendant is guilty in manner and form as charged in the bill of indictment and they fix the term of his imprisonment in the **sai** **se**Penitentiary House of this State to the period of ....**99**..... years. Whereupon the Court proceeds to pass sentence, which is that the said Defendants**, Claude Robertson, Alias,** **Hermie Lee Jones, Alias,** be delivered to the Sheriff of .....**Sevier**............ County, and at the earliest convenience conveyed to the Penitentiary House of this State, and delivered to the keeper thereof, to be confined therein at hard labor for the period of .....**99**..... years, the time fixed by the Jury aforesaid; that the date of his imprisonment commence from the..**the..date..of..conviction/**.....; **November 17, 1949**

................................; that he pay the costs of this prosecution, and that execution issue. **Sentence imposed in this case will run concurrently with sentence** **imposed in case No. 1133.**

State of Tennessee, ...**Sevier**................. County

I, **H. T. Ogle** ...., Clerk of the Circuit Court of ....**Sevier**..... County, do hereby certify that the above is a true and perfect transcript of the Judgment and Sentence in the case of the State of Tennessee vs. **Claude Robertson, Alias,**..............., indictment **Hermie Lee Jones, Alias,**

for   **Murder** .... as the same appears of record in my office.

In Testimony Whereof, I have hereunto set my hand and affixed the seal of said Court, at office in the town of ...**Sevierville, Tennessee** this ......**17th**.. day of .....**November**............, 19....

.... Clerk.

.... D. C.

Chapter 9

The Defense's Decision to Plead Their Clients

As noted, Ray H. Jenkins was the best known defense attorney of the day in East Tennessee. Jenkins knew the ropes and had represented hundreds of murderers over the preceding three decades. He knew the law, he possessed an overpowering, commanding courtroom presence, and he knew juries, at least as well as any one man could know juries.

In the Perry murder case Jenkins was the lead counsel and was assisted by Erby Jenkins, his partner of many years, and O. M. Connatser of Sevierville who had represented Claude Robertson in the Ward murder case in 1941. Jenkins represented Hermie Lee and Basil Jones while Robertson on this occasion was actually represented by Sevierville attorney Clyde Bogart.

Seventeen months after his guilty plea and 99-year sentence, Hermie Lee attempted to secure his freedom through the State Board of Pardons and Paroles and by then Governor Gordon Browning. He had hired another attorney who was quoted in *The Sentinel* as saying, "since that time (of the sentencing), a confession has been made by Claude Robertson in which he takes sole responsibility for the crime." The unidentified lawyer also had three affidavits "from people who saw Jones in Kingsport on or about the time of the crime." Jones, in his interview with the parole officer, professed his innocence and related that "over his vigorous protest," his trial lawyer (Jenkins) entered a plea of guilty for him. Jones claimed that he had paid Jenkins his life savings to defend him, had no other resources to hire another attorney, and had to accept the sentence of the court.

Jenkins had tried unsuccessfully in pre-trial motions to convince Judge Shepherd to sever the Jones brothers from Claude Robertson and try them separately. He knew that his clients simply sitting at the same table with Robertson hurt his case. He knew that it had taken two and a half days to seat a jury because so many prospective jurors had already made up their minds that Robertson was guilty. He also knew that if Robertson took the stand in his own defense, it was very unlikely he would say anything that would help his clients, whether the jury believed him or not.

Once Judge Shepherd ruled on the consent search question and allowed into evidence those items found by Sheriff Whaley on the Jones property in Washington County, Jenkins knew acquittal for his clients was unlikely if he proceeded with the trial. The one thing of which Jenkins could be certain was that there were two jurors on this jury who would not vote for the death penalty if his clients were convicted. The jurors, Sam Headrick and the Reverend Burl Adams, after being seated in the jury box had informed Judge Shepherd that they were opposed to the death penalty. This meant the death penalty, which Attorney General Wolfenbarger had intended to seek, was no longer on the table and a 99-year sentence was the most severe sentence available to the judge in the event of conviction. So why not try the case? Why not take a chance if 99 years was the most they could get anyway?

First, had Jenkins tried the case, he ran the risk that both the Jones would be convicted and given the maximum sentence which he knew would be 99 years because of Headrick and Adams. If he then was successful in getting a new trial following appeal, he would no longer have

Headrick and Adams, and the death penalty, not 99 years, would be back on the table. Granted the strongest case was against Robertson and the weakest against Basil Jones, there was no guarantee any of them would escape death row if convicted in a second trial. The fact that the case against Basil Jones was weak presented Jenkins with a bargaining tool to gain his release in return for the guilty plea of Hermie Lee. Obviously, Robertson and his attorney agreed with this reasoning as well, and Robertson was not inclined to risk the death penalty in a second trial.

Chapter 10

The Accounts of Detective Magazines

Aside from daily and weekly newspapers, the only other publications available at the time to report the events at Perry's Camp in September 1949 were the monthly detective magazines that lined the magazine racks of newsstands and drug stores. These magazines had been around for a couple of decades. Normally, the covers depicted a sultry-looking, terrified, or dead woman to attract their readers. All of them dealt with death, sex, and sensational events. The detective magazines that covered the murders at Perry's Camp were no exception. The covers of three—*Timely Detective Cases, Real Detective, and Detective Cases* -- that reported these murders are pictured on the previous page.

The stories told by the detective magazines are addressed here to separate fact from fiction. Many in Sevier County and other nearby counties held on to some of these magazines and digested misleading and incorrect information. Those who didn't keep them read them and remembered what was reported in them. If they did not read the accounts in the local newspapers, the detective magazines were their only sources for information about the case.

March 1950 Issue of *Timely Detective Cases*

This issue featured an article titled "Mangled Bodies in the Tavern" by Judge Pat Lawson. No author's biography accompanied the story. There were photographs of Perry lying in his own blood, investigating officers in the kitchen, Sheriffs Whaley and Fisher, Robertson and Hermie Lee Jones, and Perry's Camp. The basic facts of the crimes and the crime scene were written with flair but at the same time were basically correct. Fairly accurate information was related regarding the victims' backgrounds and life styles as well as the initial unproductive investigative efforts. The story went astray in reporting the development and identification of the real suspects.

According to this account, Claude Robertson was developed as a suspect as a result of Sheriff Whaley's deputies screening and checking the activities "of all recent parolees." He was reported to have been spending an unusual amount of cash around Sevierville in the company of a voluptuous blonde from Johnson City (Ms. Buchanan was a brunette from North Carolina) and had negotiated a deal to buy a new car for cash. The primary source of information came from a Sevierville taxi cab driver who claimed to have chauffeured Robertson from Sevierville to Johnson City, Kingsport, and Newport carrying bags of money. Robertson, according to the taxi driver, took money to Herman Jones in Kingsport and to an unknown individual in Newport. The cab driver directed Sheriff Whaley, Chief Reagan, and Cocke County Sheriff Fisher to the Newport residence where a subsequent interview of this individual resulted in his turning over approximately $400 in silver which he had received from Robertson the same day the bodies of Perry and Law were discovered.

The article went on to say Robertson was arrested on Friday following the murders and while not confessing was very "cooperative." A search of the Jones' property yielded "several thousands of dollars hidden in the barn" … found in a pillowcase bearing "Perry's Camp." The clinching piece of evidence was a bloody footprint found at the scene of Perry's murder that was matched to Robertson.

The account closed with the guilty pleas of Robertson and Hermie Lee Jones and their 99-year sentences. No mention was made of Basil Jones.

This account made for interesting reading and sold magazines, but it was not based on the facts in the case but rather on the imagination in the mind of Judge Lawson. To begin with, the story about how Robertson was developed as a suspect may have been told by Sheriff Whaley or Sheriff Fisher, but if it was, it was told in an effort to protect the identity of Robert Gunter. Gunter almost certainly had been assured by the Sheriffs that they would do all they could to keep the heat off of him while at the same time making him understand that his testimony would be required if the case went to trial. Howard McMahan was the Sevierville taxi cab driver who hauled Robertson around, but Howard never took him outside of Sevier County. Instead, Howard drove Robertson to places where he met up with his drinking and gambling buddies, to Mosey Moore's house, and to Perry's Camp. The only cab driver that was located that had any bearing on the case was James Ledford, the Johnson City cabbie who drove Robertson from Fall Branch to Gunter's Cocke County home on September 21st. Neither McMahan nor Ledford were summoned to testify before the special grand jury on September 30th; Robert Gunter was.

The fact that Robertson fell short of confessing but was very "cooperative" was reported in the newspaper accounts. Robertson became cooperative after Joyce Buchanan failed to furnish him an alibi and Robert Gunter had put him in possession of monies taken during the robbery and murders. Robertson said he was the lookout and that the Jones' brothers were the killers. He became more cooperative following the arrests of the Jones and obviously furnished with some specificity the location of the pillow case in the barn and the fire on the Jones property. No money was found in the pillow case other than a couple of old bills no longer in circulation.

The report in this account of a bloody footprint found at the crime scene being subsequently matched to Robertson's footprint is the only report of this very incriminating evidence.

April 1950 Issue of *Real Detective*

This magazine issue carried a story titled "Knife Torture" by J. Hoyt Cummings. This version also depicted Perry on the kitchen floor, but in addition, carried a photo of

Ms. Law lying on her back dead on her bed. It also carried a picture when he was alive, a shot of Perry's Camp, and the arrest photographs of Robertson and Hermie Lee and Basil Jones with Sheriffs Whaley and Fisher.

This rendition, like *Timely Detective Cases,* was generally correct as to the details of the crimes although inconsistent in the finer details. This story like the *Timely* story was written in the style of a novel, not a news account.

Also like the *Timely* version, this story developed Robertson in the same manner, i. e., checking the files of six ex-convicts. He was arrested on the Friday following the murders based on the fact that he had been showing a bankroll around town and had bought a new car. Robertson told Sheriff Whaley he had been with a red-haired woman in Johnson City the night of the murders and that she would support his alibi. This woman would later fail to furnish Robertson the alibi he needed. In the interim, however, Sheriff Whaley contacted the warden at Brushy Mountain State Prison, where Robertson had been incarcerated on the voluntary manslaughter conviction, to determine who he associated with while there. The warden allegedly told Whaley his cellmate was Herman Jones from Fall Branch near Johnson City.

On the Thursday following the murders, a witness reported having seen a taxi cab drop a man at Perry's Camp on Monday evening, and as a result, cab companies in Sevierville and Knoxville were being canvassed in an effort to locate a fare matching this information. When their attention turned to Johnson City cab companies, it was determined that Basil Jones had taken a cab from his home in Fall Branch to Perry's Camp on the evening of the murders. Following his arrest, Basil furnished a statement which was shown to his brother, Hermie Lee, after he was taken into custody, and admissions by both resulted in the recovery of physical evidence at their home tying them to the Perry's

Camp murders. Following these developments, Robertson allegedly began to talk and insisted he "had merely put the finger on Perry for the Jones boys."

Several incidents of misstatement of facts and pure fiction can be found in this article. Sheriff Whaley, if he called the warden at Brushy Mountain never learned that Robertson's cellmate was Hermie Lee Jones. Jones was not incarcerated at Brushy Mountain until his conviction in the Perry case; he and Robertson were, however, both in the Federal Correctional Institute at Ashland, Kentucky at the same time.

Also, this rendition reported that a witness saw a taxi cab drop a man at Perry's Camp the evening of the murders and that a subsequent canvassing of cab companies in Sevierville, Knoxville, and finally Johnson City, revealed that Basil Jones had taken a cab from his home in Fall Branch to Perry's Camp that evening. The Jones brothers never furnished statements admitting their involvement or where damning physical evidence could be found at their home. According to this account it was then that Robertson began to talk.

The next to last paragraph reveals how ludicrous most of the information reported in this article really was. The last paragraph reads ... "Basil Jones had missed connections with the others and had taken a cab to get in on the robbery."

This article, although published six months after their arrests, concludes with the indictment of Robertson and the Jones brothers. There is no mention of the resolution of the charges.

Had the writer, Cummings, been energetic enough to check on it, he would have found that Basil Jones was released after his brother and Robertson had pled guilty and received a 99-year sentence. Had any of the information about Basil in this article been accurate, Attorney General Wolfenbarger would never have agreed to Basil's release.

March 1958 Issue of *Detective Cases*

This account was published almost nine years following the murders and the convictions of Claude Robertson and Hermie Lee Jones at a time when television had put most such magazines out of business. Titled "Horror at the Summer Camp," and written by a Neil Wythe, this was a re-hash of *Timely's* "Mangled Bodies in the Tavern" tale. The story did generate one new and previously unreported unique fact. Following is one of the closing paragraphs:

"As the last juryman was seated, Claude Robertson and Herman Lee Jones stood suddenly and asked to be allowed to plead guilty as charged. 'We throw ourselves on the mercy of the court,' they said in unison."

Chapter 11

The Time Line – What Really Happened

Since the only contemporaneous accounts of the events that occurred in the Perry's Camp murders in September 1949 that still exist are newspaper accounts, the following time line was gleaned primarily, though not exclusively, from accounts reported by the two daily Knoxville newspapers, *The Knoxville Journal* and *The Knoxville News-Sentinel*. Most of the details came from statements made by police authorities, largely by Sevier County Sheriff J. Roy Whaley and Cocke County Sheriff Charles Fisher. Many of the details were taken from the testimony of Sheriff Whaley, the only witness to testify in the Perry case at trial prior to the defendants changing their pleas.

The trial of Claude Robertson, Hermie Lee Jones, and Basil Buford Jones was covered for *The News-Sentinel* by 29-year-old Carson Brewer, in his fifth year with the paper at that time. Brewer would write another 35 years for *The News-Sentinel*, author several books about the Great Smoky Mountains, and establish himself as a noted conservationist. His accounts of the trial, in particular, the testimony of Sheriff Whaley were detailed and concise and contained a number of direct quotes from all involved in the trial. For these reasons Brewer's accounts of the trial were used exclusively in ferreting out the details from Whaley's testimony. Some of the details of the searches of the Jones' property in Washington County were found in the *Kingsport*

Times which were not found in *The News-Sentinel* or in any other sources.

Monday, September 19th
10:45 p. m.

Claude Robertson and Hermie Lee Jones with Basil Jones driving Hermie Lee's Plymouth sedan pull into Perry's Camp after having parked Robertson's car, a borrowed car, off the road a mile or so down Highway 71 toward Pigeon Forge. Claude and Hermie slip out of the car and Basil drives on past. The restaurant is dark but the door is open. They tip-toe quietly into the kitchen where a light is on, and someone is moving around. They surprise Charlie Perry, gain control of him, and are able to wrestle him into a chair, and are trying to tie his hands behind him with the cord they brought with them.

While struggling with Perry in an effort to totally restrain him, Josie hears the commotion downstairs and started down the steps when she realized what was happening. She turned and started running back up the steps in an effort to reach a loaded shotgun (or more likely a loaded pistol she kept under her pillow) visible through a partially open closet door. Before she made it to the closet, Claude grabs her, forces her across the bed and stabs her twice—both times through the heart. He returned downstairs to help Hermie Lee with Perry, who is fighting and hitting Jones with his fist, and hit him on the head with a wooden stool in the kitchen to render him semi-conscious. Perry was 70 years of age but over six feet tall, weighed 200-220 pounds, and was still pretty strong.

Robertson demanded that Perry tell them where he kept his money but Perry refused to say anything. Robertson began slashing Perry's face and chest with the knife, and when he did not get the response he was looking for, he started burning Perry's bare feet with a lit cigarette, then matches. When he could stand no more, Perry relented and told them where some $8,000 was hidden. After gathering the cash, Robertson stabbed Perry in the left neck area and blood began to squirt.

11:30 p. m.

They were preparing to slip out the back door to meet up with Basil when they heard someone at the front door. They soon realized that there were two, three, or maybe as many as five men in the restaurant who had turned on the light and were making a phone call for help. They had run out of gas.

The men who had stopped to call for help heard a slight noise in the rear of the building. The noise they heard was one of three things: Robertson and Jones easing out the back door; Perry getting into a nearby clothes hamper to retrieve Josie's slip to put around his neck in an effort to stop the bleeding; or Perry's body sliding out the chair and onto the floor, the latter of which was the most probable. While inside the men had noticed a car passing by very slowly twice, first in one direction, then the other. As they were leaving the restaurant a car again came by and turned toward Gatlinburg. There were three occupants in the car. Basil Jones, the lookout, had picked up Robertson and his brother.

11:45 p. m.

Robertson and the Jones, because they had been seen in the car, decided to go to Washington County together rather than double back and retrieve Robertson's car and risk being seen by this group again. They knew from the phone conversation that these men were headed to Knoxville via Pigeon Forge and Sevierville, not to Gatlinburg. The trio traveled to the rural Jones property where the Jones lived with their mother.

1:15 a. m.

Upon arrival at the Jones residence just outside of Fall Branch, they went to the barn where Claude and Hermie Lee removed their blood-splattered clothes, put them in a pile nearby, and burned them. They split the money as agreed, and one of them hurriedly hid the pillow case that had contained the money in the loft. Claude left in Hermie Lee's Plymouth sedan and drove to the Dixie Hotel in Johnson City where he had been staying the past several days with Joyce Buchanan. Hermie Lee had to go work on Tuesday at Mead Corporation in Kingsport but could catch a ride with his older brother, Haynes Herbert Jones, who also worked at Mead.

Tuesday, September 20th

Claude traded Hermie Lee's Plymouth sedan for a late model or new Desoto at a car lot in Johnson City and spent the rest of the day and that night with Ms. Buchanan at the Dixie Hotel. (No retrievable records are now available to verify the Plymouth traded in on the Desoto was owned by Hermie Lee. This assumption was based on the fact Robertson did not yet own a car and Hermie Lee was the only one who did, and his car was an older model Plymouth.)

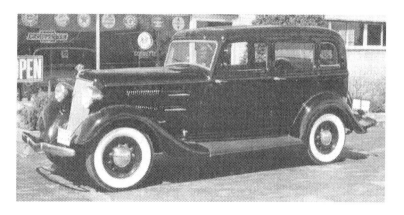

1934 Plymouth similar to Hermie Lee Jones' car traded in on Desoto

1950 Desoto

Wednesday, September 21st

     Robertson drove the Desoto from Johnson City to Jones' residence less than 30 minutes away. He had either made arrangements with Johnson City taxi driver James Ledford to follow him to Fall Branch or called Ledford after arriving at the Jones' home. Which he did depended on the availability of a telephone. Ledford drove him to Cocke County to the residence of Robert Gunter. Gunter had been incarcerated at the Federal Correctional Institute at Ashland, Kentucky at the same time as Robertson, having received his conditional release on March 27, 1948, some sixteen months before Robertson. Claude asked Gunter to either hold a bag full of money, primarily coins, or, in present-day jargon, to "launder it" for him which Gunter agreed to do. Gunter then drove Robertson to Newport that same day where Robertson paid cash with some of the money taken in the robbery for a 1940 Ford 2-door sedan. A 1940 Ford was much more Robertson's style than a Desoto. A 1940 Ford was a liquor car—a car used to run moonshine whiskey in Cocke County. A Desoto was not a car used to run liquor; it was a heavy, slow luxury car more attune to the life style of Hermie Lee Jones than Robertson.

1940 Ford 2-Door Sedan

Thursday, September 22nd

Robert Gunter had experienced prison, and like most that have been there, did not want to go back. He knew when he examined the money Claude had brought to him where it came from. The total amount of money, in coin and currency, totaled $975.35. Some of the money was in envelopes bearing the name C. J. Perry. Gunter had heard about the double murder at Perry's Camp. He knew this was a death penalty case. He also knew he didn't want any part of it. He had to decide if he wanted to risk getting caught with the money, knowing full well if Robertson got caught he'd snitch him off to try and save his own hide. But if Gunter turned Robertson in, he would have to worry about Robertson coming after him.

Gunter decided to contact Cocke County Sheriff Charles Fisher to see what could be worked out. After Gunter told his story to Fisher, the sheriff told him he would not be prosecuted but would have to testify against Robertson if the case went to trial. Gunter agreed. (Gunter was called as a grand jury witness when the case was indicted.)

Sheriff Fisher relayed the information from Gunter to Sheriff Whaley.

Friday, September 23rd

Sheriff Whaley obtained an arrest warrant for Robertson early in the day and then spent the rest of the day, along with the assistance of officers in Sevier, Cocke, Knox, and Blount Counties, looking for him. He was located late in the day at the residence of Hattie Moore Greene in Sevierville's McMahan Addition. Robertson was sitting in the 1940 Ford in front of the house when he was arrested by Sheriff Whaley and THP Patrolmen Webb and Beadle. Robertson was transported to Newport and lodged in the Cocke County Jail.

Saturday, September 24th

Robertson denied to Sheriffs Whaley and Fisher that he had given any money to Gunter to hold and that he had been with Joyce Buchanan in Johnson City on the previous Monday evening. The sheriffs drove to Johnson City where the police department had located Ms. Buchanan and detained her. Ms. Buchanan acknowledged she had spent time with Robertson and had been with him when he traded the Plymouth for the Desoto, and was with him on Tuesday evening, but that they were not together on Monday evening, the 19th. She did not know Robertson's whereabouts on that evening.

When Sheriff Whaley returned to Newport that same evening and told Robertson his alibi had not stood up, he admitted he had given the money to Gunter to hold for him and that he was present when the money was taken. He admitted to being the lookout during the robbery and identified the Jones brothers as his accomplices. Robertson informed the sheriffs that between $7,000 and $8,000 had been taken in the robbery.

Sunday, September 25th

Sheriff Whaley obtained arrest warrants for the Jones brothers and was assisted by officers from several departments in locating and arresting Hermie Lee Jones at Mead Corporation in Kingsport and Basil Jones in Fall Branch. Both were initially lodged in the Washington County Jail at Jonesborough but were subsequently taken to the Cocke County Jail. The only statement made by either of the Jones brothers in Whaley's presence was made by Hermie Lee. He admitted knowing Claude Robertson but had not seen him since he (Jones) had been released from the federal prison at Ashland, Kentucky. Upon arrival at the Washington County Jail and seeing Basil, Hermie Lee yelled and told him "keep your damned mouth shut."

Sheriff Whaley and others proceeded to the Jones property near Fall Branch where they searched the residence.

Located in an upstairs bedroom was a 45-caliber handgun like the one determined to have been stolen from Perry when he was murdered. The serial number had been filed off but there was a small dent on top of the barrel that would affect its identification as Perry's gun.

Tuesday, September 27th

Sheriff Whaley, after re-interviewing Robertson and obtaining more detailed information, returned to the Jones property and located the pillow case under a bed of hay in the loft of the barn that contained the receipt and bank deposit slip bearing Perry's name, old money, Perry's keys, and the cord used to bind Perry's wrists when he was murdered. Whaley also located the remains of the fire where Robertson and Hermie Lee had burned their bloody clothes.

Chapter 12

The Post Trial Lives of the Defendants and Their Families

The Recanting of Robertson and His Remaining Life

Claude Robertson had only been in prison three months when he furnished a statement in which he took sole responsibility for the murders of Charlie Perry and Josie Law. In a detailed affidavit dated February 29, 1950 Robertson stated he borrowed Hermie Lee Jones' car and drove the 76 miles from the Jones' home in Fall Branch to Perry's Camp by himself. He related that he had been drinking before being ordered out of the restaurant by Perry, and after arguing, Robertson killed both Perry and Law.

Why did Robertson write out such a totally ludicrous and unbelievable confession? To believe this one would have to believe that Robertson, a slightly built man who had done little during his lifetime to strengthen his body, had been able to overtake Perry, a man over six feet tall and weighing 200-220 pounds, tie him up, then stab Josie to death, then return to Perry, torture him, and then stab him to death. And, he was able to do all this before Josie could get to the shotgun, and before Perry could get the 45-caliber handgun that was found six days later in an upstairs bedroom of the Jones' residence. Jones later twice based his application for parole in part on this "confession" by Robertson.

Robertson and Jones were initially transported to Brushy Mountain State Prison at Petros following their trial. Both were very shortly thereafter, however, transferred to the State Penitentiary in Nashville during the following week. Jones was transferred back to Brushy Mountain four years later.

Brushy Mountain State Prison

According to a Robertson family descendant, Claude had been threatened and intimidated by Jones and was convinced that Jones was going to kill him or have him killed. He revealed this information to his sister, Lucy, during visits at the Nashville penitentiary.

Lucy had stuck with her brother through all of it—through thick and thin. She had put him up when he needed a place to stay. Claude was always welcome at her house and could stay as long as he liked. She always took his cigarettes, liquor, and his gun, if he was armed, but would return them to him when he left. Neither Lucy nor her husband allowed that kind of thing in their home. She tried every way she could to help Claude and encouraged other family members to do so without a great deal of success. Claude told her he made money in the penitentiary—loan-sharking, selling cigarettes, whatever—and could afford to pay a lawyer with some help. But the help never came. Lucy loved her brother unconditionally and did until he died.

Robertson would return to Sevier County twice. The first time was for the funeral of his father who died on January 2, 1954. The Tennessee Highway Patrol transported Robertson to the Knox County Jail in Knoxville on Saturday, January 3rd and then to Atchley Funeral Home in Sevierville the following morning where, in shackles and escorted, he viewed his father alone a few minutes for the last time. The family was there to see Claude but was not allowed to be with him. Only the Tennessee Highway Patrolmen were with him inside. The funeral home was surrounded with law enforcement officers. This protection was as much, if not more so, for him, than it was for those around him. Following the viewing, he was placed back in the Tennessee Highway Patrol cruiser and driven back to the Nashville penitentiary.

The Old State Penitentiary in Nashville

The second time Robertson returned to Sevier County was for his own funeral. He died at age 55 on Sunday afternoon, May 3, 1964. He was buried in the same cemetery as his parents and brother. He preceded all his nine siblings in death except Robert Marion who had died 20 years before in France.

The warden of the Nashville penitentiary, John D. Winsett, described Robertson in *The Journal* as "a model prisoner" during his almost 15 years in Nashville. Robertson had spent almost 18 and one-half years of his life in prison, and most of that for killing three people. Incredibly, however, in the killing of "Bun" Ward, a case where he laid in wait to blow him away with a shotgun, he served 19 months in state prison; in the forging and cashing of a government check for $77.94, he served 26 months in federal prison.

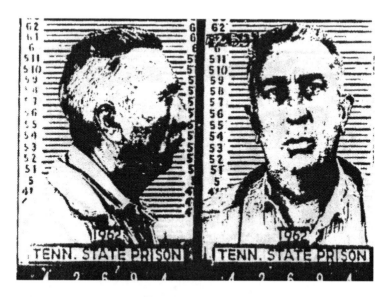

Claude Robertson at Age 53

Interestingly, neither *The Journal* nor *The News-Sentinel* disclosed a cause of death. The family was told by officials of the State Department of Corrections that Robertson died of a heart attack. He reportedly had been sitting on bleachers watching an inmate ball game when he collapsed and fell off the bleachers. Lucy never believed it, pointing out when his body was returned to Atchley's in Sevierville, there was a depression, a hole, in the side of his head the size a hammer would have made. Another sister who saw the mark attached no particular significance to it. However, a descendant of the Ward family, who went to the funeral home to make sure Robertson was dead, also told of a hole in Robertson's head, saying that it looked like a bullet wound. His death certificate, however, which was made a part of his prison file, reflects his cause of death as cardiovascular accident due to congestive heart failure and a myocardial infarction (heart attack).

In September, 1951, almost two years after arriving at the Nashville penitentiary, Robertson was afforded an inmate evaluation. Following is the verbatim summary prepared by the evaluator.

"This is a bad man, cool, calculating, poor personality, cruel, insolent and uncooperative. What information he would reveal had to be wrung from him by the interviewer. He reports he is 42 years of age, has 3rd grade education, good family background, fair employment record, stable residential history, no religious affiliation or military service and has no rationalization to offer for his crime, to which he plead guilty and states he was guilty. He has served one former state penitentiary sentence and one federal penitentiary sentence, conditionally released on the latter sentence, violated his conditional release and is now wanted as conditional release violator at the expiration of his sentence in this institution. Close custodial care is recommended. Prognosis when released very poor." (Robertson's good time release date was June 17, 2000.)

Robertson's permanent visitation record included his brother, Tip, and two of his sisters, Lucy and Eunice. His mail correspondence with family members was limited to his father, Tip, and Lucy. By far his most frequent correspondent was Ruth Allen, the younger sister of Robertson's former spouse, Reba. Claude and Ruth exchanged letters on a monthly basis for a number of years during which time she resided in Sevierville, at three different addresses in Knoxville, at two different addresses in Orange, California, and at another in El Medona, California.

Ruth Allen's relationship was recorded in Claude's prison file as "cousin?" Ruth and her husband, Alfred Perry Allen, had seven children—five boys and two girls—Phillip, James Claude, Dorothy, Harold, Wilma, Ralph, and Carl. The family moved to Orange, California in 1952. Ruth and Perry divorced in 1964 or 1965 and she later returned to Knoxville as did Wilma, Ralph, and Carl. The others stayed in California where Alfred Perry Allen died in 1967.

The last entry of significance in Robertson's Department of Corrections file indicates that in December, 1962, both he and his cellmate, identified only as a J. Myers, were re-assigned to different cells because they could not get along.

The last remnant of Robertson's prison life, a photo album, ended up in the hands of a sister following his death. This 60-year-old album, one of the old string-bound albums with black construction paper, contained 95 photographs, Most of these photographs—81—were of the Moore family, in particular, of Ruth Moore Allen and her sons and daughters. There were two photographs of Claude and Reba together, seven photographs of Robertson family members, and five photographs identified by neither the Robertson nor the Moore families. There were also three postcards dated between 1952 and 1956 from Ruth Allen. Additionally, there was a 1954 re-election card of Governor Frank G. Clement among the photographs and postcards. All the photographs, the postcards, and Clement's card were steadfastly glued to the black construction and the items had over time became inseparable. Stuffed between extra pages were three card-size religious booklets—two from the Southern Baptist Convention and one from Voice Christian Publications of California—like those regularly distributed to jail and prison populations.

The Parole of Hermie Lee Jones and Life Afterwards

Hermie Lee Jones arrived at the Tennessee State Penitentiary, Nashville four days after being sentenced by Judge Shepherd. Inasmuch as the Perry murders had been committed while he was still on federal parole for the A. W. O. L. and escape case, a hold was placed by the U. S. Marshall, Knoxville in February but was removed a year later.

Less than two years after arriving at Nashville, on the morning of August 10, 1951, he stabbed fellow inmate Richard West three times. West, of Robertson County, who was serving a 25-year sentence for the 1936 bludgeon death of his grandmother, died 13 hours later in the prison hospital. West's slaying was not reported to the Davidson County District Attorney General's office until two weeks later. The warden, Glenn Swafford, advised he had been on vacation at the time the killing occurred, but that he reported the matter immediately upon his return. Jones was charged with murder and the grand jury was scheduled to hear evidence in the case on September 10th.

West, described by prison officials as the prison's "bad boy," had drawn a dirk and advanced on a group of prisoners. When he came at Jones, the blade caught in a towel on Jones' arm, and Jones took the weapon away from

West and stabbed him. Jones was not indicted by the grand jury as it was determined he acted in self-defense.

Just three months before this killing, Jones had been denied clemency by the State Pardons and Paroles Board. Through his attorney, Richard D. Demeree of Greeneville, Tennessee, Jones had based his plea for clemency on Robertson's "confession" of February 20, 1950 in which he claimed to have murdered both Perry and Law by himself, and three affidavits from people who allegedly saw Jones in Kingsport at or about the time of the murders. Attorney General Joe Wolfenbarger, who had prosecuted Jones, publicly stated he would not recommend Jones for a pardon. On May 4th when Jones' appeal was denied by the Board he was accompanied by his attorney, his brother, and his sweetheart.

During his first 18 months at Nashville, Jones was punished for gambling and planning with other inmates to escape. In July, 1953 the discovery of a set of cell keys and 52 bullets found hidden near Jones' cell landed Jones in solitary confinement for over a year. Correction officials feared that Jones had a pistol hidden somewhere behind the walls. After being released from solitary confinement, Jones was transferred from Nashville to Brushy Mountain State Prison.

On January 26, 1965, less than nine months after the death of Robertson, then Governor Frank G. Clement commuted Jones' sentence from 99 years to life, which meant he was eligible for parole immediately. A week later, Jones was released from state custody a free man.

Jones' parole came about as a result of several factors. On October 16, 1964, a large delegation appeared before the Board of Pardons, Paroles and Probation at Brushy Mountain State Prison and testified on his behalf. A lengthy petition supporting his appeal for clemency, which included "a written statement of nine of the jurors who passed sentence upon subject," had been filed previously. Jones claimed that Robertson had borrowed his car and was driving it on the night of the murders. The reasons for the commutation continued, "Following the arrest of Robertson, the Sheriff discovered some personal effects of one of the deceased, hidden under some hay in the loft of the home of subject's mother where subject and his brother, Basil B. Jones, also resided." The document referred to Basil B. Jones as a "prominent Methodist minister," who was also a co-defendant in the case. It then detailed the statement Robertson made after arriving at the Nashville penitentiary wherein he took sole responsibility for the murders. The commutation then relates, "This subject, fearful that his preacher brother might be convicted owing to the unusual circumstances, did not take the witness stand and his brother was acquitted by agreement of the District Attorney General."

The commutation goes on to say that Jones had been a "model prisoner" for 15 years "... not having violated any of the prison rules. His aged mother and many other prominent citizens of East Tennessee testified before the Board to events, which, if true, would have exonerated this subject." The Board did not rule on Jones' guilt or innocence, but rather after a lengthy hearing, a review of the prison file, and interrogation of Jones, unanimously decided "no harm would be done society" if Jones' sentence were commuted from 99 years to life.

The reasons supporting the parole of Hermie Lee Jones had no factual basis. If nine of the twelve jurors did, in fact, sign statements supporting clemency did they, in fact, "pass sentence" on Hermie Lee Jones at the time of his trial? The jurors' names were simply listed on the verdict form. There was no trial. The jury heard opening arguments, the testimony of Sheriff Whaley, and the change of pleas— nothing else. The jury didn't decide either the guilt or innocence of Hermie Lee Jones or his sentence. Both were decided by Hermie Lee Jones. Hermie Lee Jones changed his plea from not guilty to guilty and agreed to accept a sentence of 99 years.

The statement furnished by Robertson on February 20, 1950 was most likely obtained through threats and intimidation. Its content was neither credible nor consistent with the evidence in the case. The document mentioned "personal effects" of Perry being found in the hay loft at Jones' home but offered no explanation as to how they got there. Additionally, Jones, for fear his prominent Methodist preacher brother might have been convicted, did not take the witness stand in his own defense. This contention makes no sense whatsoever. Basil Jones, charged in the same indictment with Robertson and Hermie Lee Jones, became a Baptist preacher in 1960 and was not a prominent Methodist minister at the time of his arrest for murder.

Finally, all information concerning the prison record of Hermie Lee Jones—his punishment for gambling and planning with other inmates to escape, the 52 bullets and set of cell keys found near his cell, his stint in solitary confinement, and his killing another inmate—was apparently kept from the Board. The Board's concurrence that Jones had been a "model prisoner" during his 15 years in prison was accepted in the same manner as the other reasons given to grant commutation of his sentence.

Hermie Lee Jones, when he tried to obtain a pardon or parole in 1951 based on Robertson's "confession," was interviewed by a parole officer in connection with his plea for clemency. Jones at that time blamed his attorney, Ray Jenkins, for his being in prison. He denied any knowledge of the crimes, insisted he was innocent, and over his vigorous objections, Jenkins had entered a guilty plea for him. He asserted he had no recourse other than to accept the sentence of the court.

There was no opposition to Jones' commutation and parole. When the Board heard testimony on October 16, 1964 no one was present to speak for the victims. No relatives of Charlie Perry or Josie Law were at Brushy Mountain that day. Neither was any of the judiciary from Sevier County. Sheriff Whaley was no longer in office; Ray Noland was the sheriff. Henry F. "Dutch" Swann from Dandridge, an assistant under Joe Wolfenbarger, was the District Attorney General. He had been elected following Wolfenbarger's retirement. There is no way of determining now if the Board failed to notify Sevier County authorities or if they were notified and did not respond.

Hermie Lee Jones was released from Brushy Mountain State Prison February 2, 1965 a free man—free to live out his life the way he wanted. He would live another 37 years before dying on June 22, 2001 at age 77 in Hearthstone Health Care, a nursing home in Blountville, Tennessee. He married, and although the marriage eventually ended in divorce, he had a son and a daughter. He also had a granddaughter at the time of his death. He had ten years with his mother before she died in December, 1974. He worked a factory job at Ball Metal Corporation in Greeneville, Tennessee and retired from there in 1991. Hermie Lee Jones had a relatively full life following his years in prison. He was a member of First Baptist Church in Fall Branch and was buried in the church's cemetery.

The Life of Basil Jones after the Trial until His Death

Unlike his brother, Hermie Lee, and Claude Robertson, Basil Jones got into a car with his family when he left the Sevier County Courthouse on the afternoon of November 17, 1949. He could only watch as his brother and Robertson were placed in a Tennessee Highway Patrol car that then sped off on their way to Brushy Mountain State Prison in Petros. He had spent 52 days in jail since his arrest on September 26th but would spend no more. He was going home to his own bed just outside of Fall Branch in Washington County, an hour and a half ride from Sevierville.

As a result of decisions made by his brother, Robertson, their attorneys, and the prosecutor, Attorney General Joe Wolfenbarger, he was a free man. His brother was looking at dying in prison. Hermie Lee had been sentenced to 99 years without the possibility of parole. His father had died 17 months before when Basil was barely 19. Now his brother was gone, and although he would still be able to see him, it would not be the same. Everything had happened so quickly. One minute he faced the prospect of going to prison for the rest of his life, and the next, he was going home with his mother and oldest brother, Haynes. He would work to help Hermie Lee gain parole, but it would be almost 16 years before that time would come. Basil would marry and would be raising two sons and two daughters before Hermie Lee walked away from prison.

Basil Jones married Elsie Marie Smith of Sullivan County in 1950 but continued to live in Fall Branch. He got a job with Southern Octagon Company in Kingsport and continued to farm as he had growing up. In 1956 he became convinced that he had been called to preach and began steering all his energies toward that goal. Without a high school education, raising a family, and working another job, preparing for the ministry was a difficult task. He began as a lay preacher and preached sermons at the City Mission in Kingsport and helped with funeral services at area funeral homes and churches as the third minister. He did this for several years before becoming an ordained Baptist minister and getting his first of several churches in the Holston Valley Baptist Association. He and his family moved to Rogersville where he served as pastor of Hickory Cove Baptist Church. He would later pastor First Baptist Church in Surgoinsville and East Rogersville Baptist Church. He was a member of

Shepard's Chapel Baptist Church in Rogersville when he died.

In 1974 Basil Jones experienced two of the greatest losses of his life—his 14-year-old son and his mother. In mid-August, Timothy Will Jones was with five of his friends on posted property exploring a cave. The property was located behind Hickory Cove Baptist Church where Basil was the pastor. Timothy had lain down just outside the mouth of the cave to rest while the others went inside. From 300 yards away, the 26-year-old property owner's son, using a high-powered rifle with a telescopic scope, mistook Timothy's head for a groundhog. Less than four months later, still grieving the loss of his son, his mother, who had been living with him for several years, passed away.

In November, 1988 his wife of 38 years and the mother of his children died at age 59. He later remarried Lucy Carpenter and she survived him at the time of his death at age 77 on December 8, 2007. The January 2008 issue of the *Mission-Aider*, the newsletter of the Holston Valley Baptist Association, headquartered in Jones' hometown of Rogersville, described Reverend Jones as ... "a beloved pastor, a respected fellow servant, an encourager of others in the faith, and a dedicated soul winner."

Deaths played a major role throughout the life of Basil and were the causes of the turns his life took. His father died when he was 19. At age 20, under the influence of his brother, he experienced the deaths of Charlie Perry and Josie Law, an event that had a profound effect on the rest of his life. Then the premature and tragic death of his son followed closely by the death of his mother. And then, at age 59, his wife died an early death. There had to have been times when Basil Jones thought that prison would have been easier.

The Impact on the Families

The murders of Charlie Perry and Josie Law impacted the families of both the victims and the defendants. The families of all five listened intently in the Sevier County courtroom during the four days of proceedings, in particular, the testimony of Sheriff Whaley, in mid-November, 1949. All the families were seated near Judge Shepherd on opposite sides of his bench.

Charlie Perry's family consisted of two brothers and two sisters, all in their sixties. All his siblings lived in the Chattanooga area and had no other ties to Sevier County. His father had died almost 30 years before, and his mother, almost 50 years before. His former wife, Lawson, was in Monroe County and only read newspaper accounts of the proceedings. His common-law wife, Josie, had been slain only minutes before him. He had no children. For these reasons, the greatest impact that Perry's death had on his family was their inheritance of his estate a year later. His family, of course, felt a sense of loss but not nearly as much as that felt by the Law family.

Josie's brother, Huse, and her sister, Sarah, and their spouses, all of Blount County, attended the trial every day. Josie's mother, Mary G. Cable Law, of the genealogically well-known Cable family of Cades Cove in Blount County, had died in 1944. Josie was, in fact, born in Cades Cove. Josie's daughter, whose identity and guardian is unknown to this day, was believed to be about 12 years old. She may never have known about her mother's violent death and the feelings the family endured those fall days in Sevierville. Following the sentencing of Claude Robertson and Hermie Lee Jones, Huse Law declared that he would never step foot in Sevier County again, and according to his granddaughter, Vivian Law England, he never did. The Law family never received any of Josie's personal property, quilts, personal items, and the like, inasmuch as she preceded Perry in death by a matter of minutes, and consequently, her estate went to him, then to his estate. Today, other than photographs and the guest book from Rawlings-Miller Funeral Home in Sevierville, there is little left by which to remember Josie.

The Robertson family had experience at attending Claude's court proceedings and trials. Just eight years before he had been on trial for killing Bun Ward and had been in prison twice during that time. One of his supporters—his mother—had lived through the Ward killing and trial but had died between Claude's state prison term for manslaughter and his federal prison term for check forgery. His two most loyal and attentive supporters were his father, the former sheriff of Sevier County, and his sister, Lucy. Most of his other siblings had given up on him. In fact, a Robertson descendant told of another sister who said that Claude belonged in prison, that she would not have gained his release from prison if she could have done so by snapping her fingers. The Robertson family was afraid of Claude when he was drunk. When he was liquored up he was mean and abusive. He demonstrated this sort of behavior to his family for years.

After Claude was sentenced and sent to the State Penitentiary in Nashville there were few visits from any family members other than Lucy and her family. Once when Lucy was visiting Claude, she had taken him a treat of some sort –cookies, a cake, or the like—in a box which was set aside after the treat had been given to him. When she was ready to leave, she mistakenly picked up a box from the area where her box had been placed that contained some butcher knives. The guards caught the error and immediately gave her much unwanted attention. She laughed about it afterwards with her family, but there was seldom much to laugh about following the visits. A 99-year sentence with no prospects for parole was no laughing matter. Claude Robertson and his crimes would be talked about for years in

Sevier County, and most of his family wished that the talk would just go away.

The primary supporters of the Jones brothers at the trial were their mother, Mrs. Oma Jones, and their older brother, Haynes, and his wife, Reba. They had the support of their attorneys as well, but all of them were from Fall Church in Washington County some 76 miles away. They didn't know anyone in Sevier County. The end result—Hermie Lee's sentence of 99 years—had the greatest impact on his mother. She had, like Claude's mother, endured one prison sentence, but this one was different. The first was for twenty years, was commuted to six years, and he had served only two. The 99-year sentence meant he could die in prison.

His family visited Hermie Lee at Nashville and at Brushy Mountain State Prison at Petros where he spent twelve of his fifteen years until his parole in 1965. His mother would testify on his behalf at his commutation hearing at Petros in the fall of 1964. Mrs. Jones got to spend the last 10 years of her life with Hermie Lee and would see him marry and start a family.

The murders of Charlie Perry and Josie Law perhaps had the greatest impact on Basil Jones. He very likely became a minister in an effort to gain absolution for a deed that he must have wished he could erase from his memory forever.

Chapter 13

The Recollections of Sevier Countians

Previous chapters have included information about the Perry murders furnished by Sevier County residents who knew Claude Robertson and recalled specific events surrounding September 19, 1949. Included among these were Howard McMahan, the young cab driver who regularly hauled Robertson from place to place around Sevier County; J. R. Layman, a frequent patron of Perry's Camp who saw Robertson and the 1940 Ford he had purchased two days following the Perry's Camp murders; and unnamed relatives and descendants of the Robertson and Ward families.

As noted in the opening of the *Introduction*, anyone who was alive in Sevier County when these killings occurred heard about them. The following Sevier Countians whose comments were solicited by the author or his collaborator were between the ages of 5 and 24 when the murders took place. Consequently, these people have very specific and personal recollections about what occurred at that log and stone building between Pigeon Forge and Gatlinburg in the fall of 1949.

Mary Lee Thomas Bowers

Mary Lee Thomas was a sophomore majorette at Sevier County High School when the Perry's Camp murders occurred. She would later become a Knoxville Smokies baseball queen, a majorette at the University of Tennessee, and later a model, but would never forget the terrible feelings she had when she heard about the horror of those murders. This unforgettable event happened at about the time she and her friends first started driving and taking frequent trips to Gatlinburg. She and her friends always dreaded passing by the scene of that tragedy but had to do it twice every time they drove to Gatlinburg. Driving past Perry's Camp gave her cold chills for years. There was nothing else comparable to those murders that happened in Sevier County when she was growing up in Sevierville.

T. J. Cantwell

T. J. Cantwell has been involved in law enforcement in Sevier County since 1951 when he came to the county as a Tennessee Highway Patrolman. He currently serves as the Chief Deputy with the Sevier County Sheriff's Department.

Cantwell became acquainted with Sheriff J. Roy Whaley after coming to Sevier County and talked to him about the Perry case. One comment that Sheriff Whaley made that has remained with him over the years was Whaley's initial reaction to the crimes. Whaley told him that on the morning he found Charlie Perry and Josie dead, "If he could have stepped out of the sheriff's office honorably, he would have just resigned." Whaley felt this way because the likelihood of solving the case seemed so hopeless in the beginning. Of course, he went on with the case and solved it in a relatively short period of time.

Cantwell, of course, did not know Perry but Sheriff Whaley told him stories about Perry. He related the story about Perry buying shoes for those who needed them at McCookville School.

Glenn Cardwell

Glenn Cardwell, a Pittman Center High School graduate and life-long resident of Sevier County, was a freshman at East Tennessee State University in Johnson City in September 1949 when the Perry's Camp murders occurred. He, like everyone else in Sevier County, heard second-hand accounts and read newspaper articles about what had happened. The murders were widely covered whereas in today's world, such events would all but go unnoticed. He served in the U. S. Navy during the Korean War and recalled being aboard ship in the middle of the Pacific Ocean in 1951 when a shipmate came up to him with a magazine containing an article about the killings. At the time, he found it amazing that the story of those Sevier County murders had found its way to him aboard that ship in the Pacific.

Jack Conner

Jack Conner was born and raised in Sevier County and lived in Pigeon Forge. His father, Ernest, before founding Conner Motor Company, the Pontiac dealer in Sevierville, served two terms as Sevier County Sheriff from 1936 to 1940.

Conner knew Claude Robertson and his reputation for being a mean person. He recalled meeting him on the road in Pigeon Forge when he was walking home one night. Robertson was walking on the right side of the road and Conner was walking on the left. Conner got as far to left on his side of the road that he could get. He was simply scared to death of Claude (Claude was 22 years older than Jack.). As they passed one another, Jack said "Hello Mr. Robertson," and Claude responded, "What say, Mr. Conner."

Conner recalled a story his father told him about having to arrest Claude one night after getting a call from "Frog Alley" alleging that Claude had robbed a poker game. When Sheriff Conner got there and attempted to place Robertson under arrest, Claude said, "I ain't going." His dad told Claude that there was "a right way to go and a wrong way to go," but regardless which way he chose, he was going to jail. Claude got into the sheriff's car but kicked the windows out of the car on the way to the jail. Conner's father arrested Claude on several occasions (including Robertson's arrest for the murder of "Bun" Ward in July 1940) and when Jack knew his father was going to arrest Claude, he was always afraid for his father.

Jack Conner also knew Charlie Perry, but Perry would not sell him beer because he would not sell to minors. Conner always had to get someone else to buy his beer from Perry. He said "if you looked to suit Perry, he would sell to you. If not, Perry would tell you 'to get the hell out of my place.'" Most everyone, however, liked Perry.

Jack related a story about one man he knew who stopped to get beer at Perry's place. The man had been drinking and had already had too much. Perry refused to sell to him to which the man responded, "I'll just take it." While he was reaching down under the counter to retrieve his pistol, Perry told the man "you may take it now but you'll never take any more." The drunken customer got out of the place as fast as his legs would take him.

Conner recalled he was attending East Tennessee State University (ETSU) when the Perry murders occurred. When he learned of the arrests he and some other Sevier County students at ETSU all piled into a car and drove out to the Jones property just to see where it was located.

Agnes Marshall

Mrs. Agnes Marshall, who along with her husband, Mack, bought Perry's Camp in 1952, met Charlie Perry and Josie Law only once. On a night in 1948 when she was 20 years old she drove one of her brothers to Perry's Camp to buy beer. When Perry saw and talked to her brother, he refused to sell him any beer, telling her brother he had had enough to drink. Mrs. Marshall respected Perry for taking that stance. She met Josie Law, a pretty, petite, pleasant lady that night as well. She never saw them again.

She had been married a little over a year and was living in Sevierville at the time of the murders. She recalled thinking what a tragedy that event was and was in disbelief that such a thing could happen in Sevier County. At the time it happened she couldn't bring herself to come to Perry's Camp although she heard a lot people did come. After she and Mack bought Perry's Camp she never had any bad feelings about working and living there. There were a number of people, however, who did have difficulty just being there. Mack's maternal aunt, Anna Rainwater, would not visit them because of her bad feelings about the place. Mack's mother laughed at her and told her that it was not the dead she had to worry about but the living.

Carolyn Pierce McMahan

Carolyn Pierce McMahan, Sevier County Clerk and Master, although only six years old at the time and living at Seymour, has a very vivid recollection of the Perry murders and the terrifying memories they created for her. Although her father, Fred Pierce, was involved in law enforcement and served during the 1950's both as Sevierville Chief of Police and as Sevier County Sheriff, she learned details of the crimes, in particular, the torture of Charlie Perry, from sources other than him. Her dad simply never talked about

his work at home. Crimes like those now seem common-
place, but in 1949, those crimes where the most horrifying
crimes committed in Sevier County in years.

Jimmy Lee McMahan

Jimmy Lee, a life-long Sevier County resident, was a
junior at Sevier County High School in September, 1949
when the Perry's Camp murders occurred. He recalled being
in English class on the top floor of the high school that
morning when he heard sirens in the distance going up
Gatlinburg Highway from Sevierville. That same day word
spread throughout the school about the murders. McMahan
was not acquainted with the either of the victims or Claude
Robertson who was subsequently charged and convicted.

Beth Beal O'Donnell

Beth's childhood memories of the Perry murders
caused her to have nightmares for months. Although she was
only five years old when these killings occurred, she had
been to Perry's Camp with her mother and her aunt, both of
whom knew Charlie Perry and Josie Law. She vaguely
remembers Josie but has no recollection of Perry. She later
learned from her mother that Josie had commented when she
saw her that she (Beth) caused her (Josie) to miss her
daughter.

Jimmie Temple

On the Tuesday morning the bodies of Charlie Perry
and Josie Law were found, Jimmie Temple of the Temple
Milling Company in Sevierville was on his way to Perry's
Camp. Perry was a customer of Temple's who bought bran
to feed some hogs he raised in a pen near the camp. Perry
was one of several planned stops that day to take customer

orders for the mill. He had a short time earlier picked up Betty Jo Loveday in Pigeon Forge. He regularly gave Betty Jo, who worked as Dr. Schilling's nurse in Gatlinburg, a ride from Pigeon Forge to Gatlinburg on the days he made his rounds.

When they got to Perry's Camp, there was a crowd of people and several cars parked all around. As he pulled in he was met by Carson Webb, Tennessee Highway Patrolman assigned to Sevier County at that time. Carson told him Perry and Josie Law had been murdered and suggested that he go on to his other customers.

Temple related that Perry bought the bran to feed his hogs but always made sure that it was unsalted bran. For this reason Temple always suspected Perry was also using the bran to make whiskey as Perry had the reputation of selling illegal liquor at his place.

Jimmie Temple was one of the 147 townspeople, friends, and family who paid their respects to Josie Law at Rawlings-Miller Funeral Home in Sevierville the day after her body had been found and the day before her body was taken to Blount County for burial.

Steve O. Watson

Steve O. Watson, former Special Agent and Deputy Director with the Tennessee Bureau of Investigation, and currently a Deputy Chief with the Sevier County Sheriff's Department, remembers very well hearing about the Perry murder and that of Josie Law. The talk was mostly about Perry and how he was tortured, burned with cigarettes, cut with a knife about his face, his neck, and his upper body. Seven years old at the time, this was Steve's first recollection of murder. Talk of the murders went on for many years, and they are still talked about even today by those who were alive at the time.

Watson knew where Perry's Camp was located as he always passed by it when with his father on the way to Gatlinburg. At the time of the murders, and on into his youth when they would pass by, he could visualize all sorts of things from what he had been told about the murders. For years he felt frightened by just coming in close proximity to Perry's Camp. To this day he can still dredge up those vivid memories when passing by the site where Perry's Camp once stood. Over a 42 year career in law enforcement Watson has investigated many heinous murders but none of those remain in his mind as vividly as the stories of the Perry torture murder case from his youth.

Steve also remembered the death of Marion Robertson, a former Sheriff of Sevier County and the father of Claude Robertson. Claude Robertson had a reputation of being a very mean person in Sevier County and even the thought of him being brought from prison to Sevier County for his father's funeral was the talk of the county. People feared what could happen. Would he escape? Would he be turned loose on Sevier County again? These were the things going through people's minds at the time and what was being said. His return for the funeral was, of course, accomplished without incident, and he was afterwards returned to the penitentiary.

Steve observed that there have been many murder cases in Sevier County since 1949, some very heinous, but none of the cases have been remembered as well or as long as the Perry murders. He opined that murder during the time since the Perry murders has, unfortunately, become more common place and times have changed. Steve further observed that the way people accept murder now is a great deal different than in 1949 Sevier County, a rural farming community with a population who knew one another, most by first names. The Perry murders created a trauma in the county that had not been known since the White Cap murders of the turn-of-the-century.

As Deputy Chief, Watson has the responsibility of maintaining crime statistics for Sevier County. As a result he knows that Sevier County has experienced relatively few murders since 1994, and that Sevier County is for the most part a very law-abiding county. Steve also knows, as do a lot of other people, that Sevier County is simply a good place to live, to raise a family, to retire, and to enjoy the slow pace of living in a very beautiful place.

Harvey Wayland

Harvey Wayland grew up on Maples Branch five miles east of Sevierville. His father was one of two deputies that worked for Marion Robertson, Claude Robertson's father, when he was Sevier County Sheriff. He really didn't know Claude except by reputation but knew from his father that Marion would do whatever he could to keep Claude out of prison. Wayland knew some of Claude's associates on sight and by reputation including Johnny Hicks, Mosey Moore, and Ray Ward. He recalled as a youngster he and his brother were at Homer Thurman's grocery at the Hodsen Bridge located on the Old Newport Highway once when Hicks came in to buy a pack of cigarettes. A large man whose last name was Reagan "started giving Hicks some lip." Hicks hit the man one time and knocked him out cold in front of the cash register. Hicks flipped Thurman a quarter, reached over his victim to get his pack of Lucky Strike cigarettes from Thurman, and then left, leaving Reagan lying on the floor out like a light. Hicks was a neighbor of Wayland's and had the reputation of frequently getting into fights, including knife fights as evidenced by the knife scars on his face and arms.

Wayland also knew the Ward family as his wife, Peggy, was a first cousin of Glen Beal, "Bun" Ward's brother-in-law. He knew too that the Ward family always felt that Claude Robertson was convicted of voluntary manslaughter in the ambush killing of Bun rather than premeditated first degree murder because Marion paid off the judge and/or member(s) of the jury. Wayland has done some investigation into this matter on his own and has never found any evidence to support a payoff or jury tampering. No question but that Bun's murder was pre-meditated as Claude went home and got a gun and returned to Ward's home where he laid in the brush and waited on him. The two had been in a poker game earlier and Bun had caught Claude cheating and "worked him over a little." Bun Ward was known to be tough and a good fighter.

Of course, the charging of Claude Robertson and the Jones brothers with the murders of Perry and his housekeeper was big news in Sevier County at that time. Although the trial was short-lived, it drew capacity crowds to the courthouse in Sevierville.

Chapter 14

The Recollections of Mosey Moore's Nephews

Harold V. Allen

Harold V. Allen's mother was Ruth Moore Allen, sister of Moses "Mosey" Moore, and his father was Alfred Perry Allen from the Boyd's Creek area of Sevier County. His aunt was Reba Moore, who first married Claude Robertson, then Herbert Martin. Claude and Reba had married when they were both very young and did not stay married very long. Reba was a strikingly good-looking woman. She "hustled" at a club in New Orleans, and that is where she met Herbert. Claude remained close to the Moore family over the years and was a partner in crime with his Uncle Mosey.

Harold is one of seven children in his family. The oldest was Phillip, then James Claude, then Dorothy, then him, then Wilma, Ralph, and Carl. His older brother, James Claude Allen, was named after Claude Robertson. His mother never explained why she did that. She was close to Claude and corresponded regularly with him—more than anyone else—after he went to the penitentiary in Nashville for the murder of Charlie Perry and his housekeeper in 1949. His mother had attended every day of Claude's trial in Sevierville. His brother, "Jimmy," or "J. C.," as he was called in the family, always joked that being named after Claude Robertson was his "claim to fame." Jimmy, like he and their father, worked as an electrician. Jimmy, of Grand

Junction, Colorado, died in January, 2008 at Lake Havasu, Arizona at age 73.

Harold moved with his family in 1952 to Orange, California. His mother and he visited Claude at the Nashville penitentiary while en route to California. He recalled paying a quarter to tour the penitentiary and got to see the electric chair. He was told during the tour that the seven cells on death row were each used one night by an inmate scheduled for electrocution. When the scheduled execution of a condemned man was a week away, he was placed in the first cell the first night, then the second cell the second night, and so on. He would then spend his last night in the cell next to the room with the electric chair in it. He doesn't know to this day if that was true or not but thought it made an interesting story to tell. Harold also recalled that the inmates made small replicas of the electric chair for a dollar. When asked if he bought one, he laughingly responded, "No, I didn't have a dollar."

Harold visited Claude Robertson with his mother once more. On this occasion, his first cousin, Jim Moore, Jr., the son of his mother's brother, was with them. They were returning to California after having been back to Tennessee following the death of Jim's father in November, 1953. Harold laughed when he remembered that he and Jim went to the women's side of the penitentiary for a tour and "they ran us off." Harold was 16 years old in 1953; his cousin, Jim, was 15.

Harold recalled that Claude made his mother a braided brass necklace at the penitentiary. He still has a picture of his mother wearing this necklace.

Claude spent his entire time at the Nashville penitentiary but Jones was moved to Brushy Mountain Prison after it became apparent he was going to attempt to kill Robertson. Jones was after Claude because he had implicated his brother and him in the robbery and murders, and Jones wanted revenge for Claude "ratting him off." Harold learned of this from his mother who was told of Jones' intentions by Claude.

Harold's knowledge of Claude Robertson and his criminal activities came from being a part of the Moore family, in particular, being the nephew of Mosey. Had Mosey Moore not been his uncle, he would not have had anything to do with him. Much of what he knew about the activities of Mosey and Claude Robertson he learned from his uncle. As a result he knows that Mosey and Claude pulled some armed robberies together and also bootlegged together on the Tennessee River. He recalled one funny story Mosey told him when they were about to be raided on the liquor-running boat. They hurriedly threw the liquor overboard, and after no evidence was found by law enforcement, Mosey held Claude upside down by his feet while Claude tried to retrieve the liquor.

In about 1947 Claude and Mosey got drunk and Claude almost killed Mosey on Sutherland Avenue in Knoxville. Claude hit Mosey with an ax on the head and left him for dead. Mosey got up and walked about 90 feet to a telephone and called his own ambulance. Mosey never reported this assault to police. He was afraid Claude would either kill him or turn him in for some of the criminal activities in which they had been involved together.

Claude talked to Mosey about the murder he had committed several years before the Perry murder. Claude killed the man after he had been caught cheating in a poker game. Claude went home and got a shotgun, then laid in the brush along the road and blew him away. Mosey quoted Claude to Harold as having asked Mosey, "Would you think a man could yell after his heart had been shot out?"

According to Mosey, Claude Robertson always had his sights set on being "a big-time criminal." Also, according to Mosey, Robertson was caught for killing Perry because he was running his mouth and throwing money around. He bought a car in Newport and two handguns with the money from the robbery. Claude liked "showing off." Harold saw this attitude when he visited Claude in Nashville. He gave him the impression he liked being in prison because it made him feel like a bad man that should be feared.

Harold has lived all his adult life in California. His mother and father divorced in either 1964 or 1965, and his mother subsequently returned to Tennessee. His father died in 1967 and his mother in 1986. Before moving to California he and his family lived in the Lonsdale area of Knoxville as did Mosey. He recalled that Mosey and Jimmie Moore, Sr. worked for an Ike Joffe at a shoe repair shop on South Central Avenue in Knoxville.

James R. Moore, Jr.

James R. "Jim" Moore, Jr., whose father was Ruth Moore Allen's brother, knew his Uncle Mosey and Claude Robertson well growing up. He knew Claude Robertson was "a cold-blooded killer" who never showed any remorse for the things he did. Claude had been married to his Aunt Reba and knew that they still had feelings for one another even after she divorced him and married Herbert Martin. Reba worked at the "Puppy Dog Club" in New Orleans as a "bar girl" and that is where she met Herbert.

His first recollection of Claude Robertson was when he was only two years old. It is now difficult for him to remember what he saw himself and what he was told by others in the family. He knows that Claude came to his (Moore's) house on the night he killed "Bun" Ward. At that time his family was living in a rented house on Possum

Hollow Road (Ridge Road) in Runyon Addition in Sevierville. Claude hid the murder weapon, a shotgun, at that house that night. Jim's recollection was he put it in a well or cistern that house shared with one or more other houses. Moore feels certain the shotgun has never been recovered.

Moore knows from conversations he had with his Uncle Mosey and from just being around him and Claude that they drank, bootlegged, gambled, and caroused together in Newport, Knoxville, and other places. They also committed several armed robberies along with two other men, one from Gatlinburg, and the other, from Blount County. He knows that they pulled an armed robbery somewhere "up north" (possibly Kentucky) during which Claude killed the victim.

When Claude was arrested for the murder of Charlie Perry and his housekeeper, he was at the house of Moore's Aunt Hattie on Railroad Street in "Frog Alley." Claude was out front calling for Mosey to come out. Mosey was hiding in the house because he knew Claude intended to kill him. Claude believed Mosey was going to turn him in on the robbery-homicide that had occurred "up north" sometime during the mid-1940's. Mosey's parents, Bill and Ida Moore (Jim's grandparents), lived next door to Hattie at the corner of Railroad Street and McMahan Avenue, but Mosey lived in the Lonsdale area of Knoxville, not in Sevierville. In fact, Mosey lived immediately next door to Ruth and her family on Lantana Lane. He operated his own shop repair shop on Tennessee Avenue in Lonsdale.

Moore volunteered that Mosey, Claude, and the others they ran with were all "bad news" but opined that Claude was the worst of the bunch. Mosey was actually scared to death of Claude, and Mosey was no saint. The scariest conversation he ever had with his Uncle Mosey occurred when Mosey drove him to a business off Western Avenue in Knoxville owned by an Ike Joffe. The business was located next door to Royal Brass, Inc. Mosey told him that Joffe had a safe full of money in that business and other items of value. Mosey asked him if he would be interested in helping him rob Joffe, but pointed out that he (Mosey) would have to kill Joffe if they did because Joffe knew him. Moore told Mosey real quick that he wanted nothing to do with it.

Mosey also bootlegged liquor on the river in Sevierville. At one time Mosey kept a small houseboat tied up at the swinging bridge which was located above the old dam and behind where the bus terminal was at one time. Mosey had a line tied to the liquor which he lowered in the water. The other end of the line was tied to a post on the bank draped over the post making the line taunt. He kept a hatchet stuck in the post. This set up allowed him to cut the liquor loose if he saw the law coming.

Moore went with Mosey once to get a load of liquor. Mosey drove up into Jones Cove in Sevier County and pulled up to a house. Moore has no idea who lived there or who the two men were that was there. Mosey and he got out of the car and they sat on the porch while the two men took the car and drove out of sight. After a while they returned, Mosey paid them, and without looking in the trunk, they got in the car and left. The trunk, of course, was full of what Mosey had bought.

There were some funny stories. Jim recalled that Mosey operated a "floating crap game" and also had a shooting gallery at one time. The short-barreled rifles fired .22 caliber "shorts." Mosey fell asleep once behind the curtain, and someone accidentally shot him. He recalled another funny story that involved his Aunt Reba. She once drove a 1938 LaSalle to her parent's house from New Orleans and left it when she returned to New Orleans. The LaSalle was a four-door sedan, black, with covered spare wheels mounted in both front fenders. It was a beautiful car which he assumed was in his Aunt Reba's possession without the owner's permission. After Reba went back to New Orleans, Mosey got drunk and sold the LaSalle for $50. Reba was really upset when she found out what Mosey had done.

Mosey Moore died in 1986 leaving behind two sons, Donnie and Billy, whom he has not seen since Mosey's funeral. Jim Moore has lived most of his life in Sevier County and has worked in law enforcement.

Chapter 15

The Similarities with the White Cap Murders

Between 1892 and 1896 a vigilante group known as the "White Caps" came into existence in Sevier County. This illegal clandestine group came about as a result of the discontent and impatience of some citizens with the way the court system was dealing with violators and undesirables. Initially the White Caps consisted of elected officials and even judges and were supported financially by the county's most affluent residents. As time passed the White Caps became a haven for criminals and other questionable characters and their activities got out of control. A second vigilante group, the "Blue Bills," was formed to counteract the illegal acts of the White Caps. Although the Blue Bills were somewhat successful in helping bring down the White Caps, the incident that really caused their demise was the murder of a couple, William and Laura Whaley, on December 28, 1896 by two White Caps, Pleas Wynn and Catlett Tipton.

The Whaleys were murdered because Laura Whaley defied an oath she had taken to conceal a deceitful White Cap technique. She had been extorted to perform threatening acts toward others on behalf of the White Caps. They had been pulled from their beds at night and shot gunned at point blank range, blowing their brains out onto the floor. She fell over her husband and a huge pool of blood collected on the floor of their humble cabin home. An estimated 500 mourners came to their home to view the crime scene. After seeing and hearing of this tragedy, the citizenry of the county decided to stand up to the White Caps, decided to turn things around, and no longer tolerate the lawlessness of this group. The Whaley killings afforded the law-abiding people of Sevier County the opportunity to do that.

Unbeknownst to Wynn and Tipton, Laura Whaley's sister was an eye-witness to the murders and identified them the next day and at the trial. Tipton further incriminated himself when he testified he was with Wynn the night of the murders. A judge had been brought in from outside the county to eliminate the White Caps' influence on the trial. The convictions were appealed but upheld and on July 12, 1899 Wynn and Tipton were hanged in the Sevier County Jail yard where a gallows had been built for the occasion. Both were baptized in the West prong of the Little Pigeon River before being hanged. A huge crowd gathered for the baptisms and the hanging just as they had for the trial when they were convicted.

A third person, Bob Catlett, also a White Cap, was charged with having paid Wynn and Tipton to kill the Whaley couple. Catlett's influence was such that his trial was relocated to Hamblen County (Morristown) where he was tried and acquitted. This occurred even though Wynn and Tipton confessed and testified against Catlett. Even so, this case ended the White Cap era and vigilante justice in Sevier County.

The White Cap murders remained the most appalling crimes ever committed in Sevier County, at least, in the minds of Sevier Countians, until the Perry's Camp murders. Reference would be made to these murders committed over 50 years earlier in the Knoxville newspapers from the time the Perry's Camp bodies were found until sentences were pronounced. Even the presiding judge, the Honorable George R. Shepherd, made reference to the White Cap murders during the course of the 1949 court proceedings.

Ironically, Pleas Wynn's father, E. M. Wynn, served two terms as Sheriff of Sevier County from 1886 to 1890. Pleas worked as a jailer for his father during the last term. Additionally, Pleas' first cousin, J. W. Wynn, was Sheriff of Sevier County from 1916 to 1920.

The adage that history often repeats itself appears to be true when comparing the similarities between the murders of William and Laura Whaley in December, 1896 and the murders of Charlie Perry and Josie Law in September, 1949. Aside from being gruesome, sickening, and sensational, the murders of both couples paralleled the other in several other ways.

First, both were murders of married couples. The Whaley's marriage was recognized under the laws of the state while that of Charlie and Josie was recognized under a common law union. The Whaley's, like the Perry's, were murdered on the same evening within minutes of each other and in each other's presence. All four of the victims knew their attackers.

The motives were strikingly similar as well; the murders were committed to avenge an act or acts of another person or person(s). The White Caps, as in other previous actions, used Pleas Wynn and Catlett Tipton to avenge a perceived wrong or moral misdeed committed by Laura Whaley. Claude Robertson avenged several confrontations and incidents of combativeness that had occurred between Perry and him over several years, including Perry putting Robertson out of his place several times, Perry's support of the Ward's in the prosecution of Robertson for the killing of "Bun" Ward, and another previous disagreement known only to those who went to their graves with its knowledge.

In addition, the primary killer in each of the murders—Wynn and Robertson—resembled each other in a couple of different ways. Both men came from well-known families in Sevier County. Wynn's father had served two terms as Sevier County Sheriff while Robertson's father had previously served three terms in the same office.

Oddly enough, the West prong of the Little Pigeon River was also a common ingredient in these two cases. This river, which is fed by the creeks and streams in the Great Smoky Mountains, and flows from the Sugarlands through Gatlinburg, Pigeon Forge, and Sevierville, eventually emptying into the French Broad, played a part in all four murders. In the White Caps murders both Pleas Wynn and Catlett Tipton, before being hung, were taken to this river that ran behind the jail where the gallows awaited them, and were baptized. The Perry murders occurred in a dwelling on the banks of the same river some 10 miles upriver. It was believed the river washed the blood of the Perry's from the knife used to stab them to death. This murder weapon was never located, and it was theorized it had most likely been thrown in the river.

The Baptisms

Both the Whaley murders and the Perry murders were extremely upsetting to all law abiding citizens in the county. The trials of those responsible drew packed crowds to the Sevier County Courthouse and courtroom seats were at a premium. Both trials were historic events that were long remembered and compared one to the other.

Finally, there were similarities in the punishment of the offenders even though both defendants in the Whaley case were executed and no one in the Perry case was put to death. Both of these double homicides were death-penalty cases. One was carried out; the other one was not. However, the convicted defendants in both cases received the maximum sentences available.

The Gallows

The death penalty would have been sought in the Perry case had that option been available. Death was not an option because of the two jurors opposed to capital punishment being erroneously seated on the jury. Claude Robertson and Hermie Lee Jones received the maximum penalty that could be imposed upon them—99 years. There was no opposition to the death penalty among the jurors who heard the evidence against Pleas Wynn and Catlett Tipton.

The punishment for Wynn and Tipton was swift and final when imposed, but two and one-half years separated the crimes from their sentences due to their appeals. Since no appeal was available to Robertson and Jones, their sentences were imposed immediately and both were transported to prison the same day they were sentenced.

Chapter 16

The Most Heinous Sevier County Crimes Since the Perry's Camp Murders

During the next half century that followed the Perry murders, like the half century that preceded them, there were more violent crimes precipitated by robbery in Sevier County. These crimes rocked the community in much the same way the Perry murders had. Sevier County was an area of beauty, a place to vacation and relax, and a place to enjoy family and friends, not one associated with unthinkable crimes. Like any area that experiences growth, crime is a part of that growth. More people, more business, more money, all create more opportunities for criminals to prey on the innocent.

Perry's Camp was the first tourist court of its kind in Sevier County. Such accommodations for visitors grew as attractions, shops, and restaurants grew. One of the first such attractions was Rebel Railroad that opened in Pigeon Forge in 1961. Five years later this park, which eventually became Dollywood, was renamed Goldrush Junction and in 1977, it became Silver Dollar City. That year also brought with it another multiple-homicide robbery that again shook the county. Before this tragedy and Silver Dollar City came about, however, a double homicide occurred on Thanksgiving Day, 1970 in a part of the county not so directly affected by the growth of tourism.

The Murder of Chan and Glennie Teaster

Chan and Glennie Teaster lived at Cosby in southeast Sevier County at the Cocke County line in an area historically associated with the manufacture and distribution of moonshine whiskey, a reputation made even more popular in 1958 following the release of the movie "Thunder Road" starring Robert Mitchum. This movie, set in the mountains around Cosby, played to a packed-house for ten weeks at the theater in Newport, the county seat.

The gruesome murder of Chan and Glennie Teaster in their modest home next to Baxter's apple orchard on Thanksgiving night 1970, however, was not about whiskey or its notorious thunder road. The shotgun blasts that took off half their heads exposed the coldest, most evil side of the human psyche and allowed the killers to make off with the money in Chan's wallet and Glennie's purse. Chan was rumored to carry a substantial amount of cash.

Chan and Glennie, 67 and 61, respectively, had retired for the evening when they heard a knock at the door. Chan got up, donned his bib overalls, buttoned only one strap, and barefooted, answered the knock. He and Glennie, like Charlie Perry and Josie Law, knew their killers. Chan sat down in his rocking chair and lit a cigarette. Before he could finish it, both he and his wife died the most violent deaths imaginable—Chan in his chair and Glennie in their bed with the sheet pulled up to her neck. The killers retrieved their spent shells. The wadding from one of the shells was the only piece of physical evidence found when the bodies were discovered by a milk customer two days later. Upon leaving the killers tried unsuccessfully to burn down the Teaster's home around them by throwing a lit oil lamp down in the living room but papers dampened by cut flowers prevented the fire from igniting. The Teaster's home had no electricity.

A 28-year-old TBI Agent with two years with the agency by the name of Steve O. Watson was the primary investigator in the Teaster case. Some 17 suspects would be interviewed and 21 polygraph examinations would be conducted. A witness who showed deception on the lie-detector would 10 years later relate having heard shots and then seeing three men in the vicinity of the Teaster home leaving in a car. Two of these three men were subsequently identified but there was insufficient evidence to charge them.

In May, 2006 Watson was interviewed about these unsolved murders by WBIR, Knoxville's NBC television affiliate, and in recounting the investigation was quoted as saying, "To be able to solve this case would be the highlight of my career." Also interviewed at that time was Mildred Teaster, Chan's sister-in-law, who recalled the affect on the family. Mrs. Teaster related, "I remember it being so devastating to all of us. We just didn't know what to think about anybody who would go into their home and do that."

Hardly a day has passed since November 28, 1970, the day the Teaster's mutilated bodies were discovered, that the vision of these heinous murders has not entered Watson's mind. He still today cannot tolerate the smell of Lysol spray, the deodorizer he used at the crime scene all those years ago. Solving the Teaster case would grant Watson the consolation and closure needed to shut the door to a long and distinguished law enforcement career. In Steve's words … "In the end the case will be dealt with, if not on this earth in a court of law, then in the court of God."

Robbery of the Kodak Branch of the Citizens National Bank

On Saturday morning, April 9, 1977 the Kodak Branch of the Citizens National Bank was robbed by two men who killed three employees and one customer during the robbery. The bank, located on Highway 66, was housed temporarily in a mobile home with a wooden facade. The victims were identified as Hugh Kyle Beeler, 61, the branch manager who lived in Knoxville; Linda Kay Davis, 24, a bank teller from Kodak; Earl G. Underwood, 57, a bank customer from Kodak; and Harriet Swaggerty, 31, also a bank teller from Kodak. All were shot in the head. Beeler, Davis, and Underwood died at the scene; Mrs. Swaggerty died later at Baptist Hospital in Knoxville.

That afternoon the FBI received information from a confidential source that George William Brady and Leroy Marshall were responsible for the bank robbery and murders. Marshall was located in Newport that same evening and Brady was stopped by a Sevier County Deputy Sheriff early the following morning. Both were interrogated by the FBI. A search of Brady's car resulted in the seizure of all of the bait money taken from one of the tellers during the robbery and a .38 caliber pistol subsequently determined to have been the weapon used to fire several of the bullets recovered from the victims' bodies. (Bait money is money in tellers' drawers bearing previously-recorded serial numbers.) The search of Brady's person when arrested located an additional $500 of bait money hidden in his shoes.

Marshall had earlier that day given a female relative a bag containing $2,510 and when she asked where he got the money, he said, "Haven't you heard of the Sevier County Bank?" When the bag and a gun were recovered by the FBI the following day, three bait bills from the robbery were included among the money. This gun was determined through ballistics not to have been the second gun used to commit the murders. The second murder weapon was never recovered. A metal box taken during the robbery was subsequently recovered from the banks of the Pigeon River in Cocke County and, according to Brady's daughter, was discarded there by Marshall and her father. A witness waiting for the bank to open identified Marshall as the man who asked him prior to 9:00 o'clock that morning what time the Kodak bank opened. One of Brady's friends employed at a Pigeon Forge hotel was contacted by Brady the night of the robbery at the hotel, and Brady asked him to go to California with him for six months to two years. There was plenty of evidence with which to indict and convict Brady and Marshall of robbing and slaughtering those four innocent people inside that bank.

Brady and Marshall were convicted in both U. S. District Court in Knoxville and in Sevier County Circuit Court and received the maximum sentences available in both jurisdictions. Each received a federal sentence of 99 years and a state sentence of 416 years. Their convictions were upheld by the U. S. Sixth Circuit Court of Appeals on April 6, 1979, just three days short of the second anniversary of the crimes.

Growth and prosperity in Sevier County had brought about branch banking, which was convenient, but which was also extremely vulnerable.

The Rocky Top Murders

On Saturday evening, September 13, 1986, the same year that Silver Dollar City became Dollywood, two employees of the Rocky Top Village Inn in Gatlinburg, night clerk Melissa "Missy" Hill and security guard Troy Dale Valentine, were brutally murdered during a robbery. Ms. Hill was stabbed 18 times, her throat was cut, and she was shot in the head. Valentine was hit on the head, stabbed around the neck, and shot between the eyes.

A handwritten note, apparently written by an uneducated individual and/or one of diminished capacity, expressing remorse for committing the murders was found in a Maggie Valley, North Carolina phone booth along with a pocket knife belonging to Ms. Hill. These clues along with good, hard police work by Gatlinburg Police Detective Bud Parton and the assistance of Atlanta police subsequently led to the arrest of a weird and somewhat demented foursome that included Edward "Tattoo Eddie" Leroy Harris; Joe DeModica; Rufus Doby, also known as Ashley Silvers; and Kimberly Pelley. Harris, a drifter from Atlanta whose nickname was derived from the more than 134 tattoos on his body, and DeModica, a homosexual, had served time together in Georgia. Doby was DeModica's transvestite lover. Pelley, a homeless country girl, was Harris' heterosexual partner.

Harris' case came to trial in Sevier County Circuit Court in Sevierville in May 1988. DeModica turned state's evidence and pinned the murders on Harris and Pelley. There was no physical evidence linking Harris or the other three to the slayings. All had given hand writing exemplars and all but Harris had been excluded as having written the note found in the phone booth. A hand writing expert failed to conclusively conclude that Harris had written the note and asked for more samples. Harris refused to furnish additional exemplars; however, a former girlfriend from Atlanta testified she taught Harris to read and write and identified the handwriting in the note as that of Harris. Harris, based largely on DeModica's testimony, was convicted of armed robbery and two counts of premeditated first degree murder; he received a life sentence for the robbery and two death sentences for the murders. Both Pelley and DeModica were subsequently convicted and received life sentences. Doby entered a guilty plea and received a lesser sentence.

The death sentence meted out by the Harris jury was the first since the White Cap murders. But for an oversight in questioning prospective jurors, this sentence would have been the third death sentence since Pleas Wynn and Catlett Tipton were hung. In all likelihood Claude Robertson and Hermie Lee Jones would have otherwise been the second and third death sentences. A major difference between the sentences imposed on Wynn and Catlett and that imposed on Harris was the executions. The White Cap sentences were carried out on the gallows built for that purpose in the jail yard. Harris' death sentence was never carried out. Although Harris' initial appeals were denied, he was in June 2002 granted relief. Based on his claim that death constituted cruel and unusual punishment for a person of his mental retardation, his death sentence was set aside.

The Rocky Top murders gained national notoriety. Gatlinburg was known as a peaceful and quaint vacation resort town in the Smokies, but this case caused it to be painted as unsettling and fearful. In January 2001 the A&E network's "City Confidential" aired an hour-long feature called "Smoky Mountain Nightmare," which did nothing to restore public confidence in the vacation Mecca and the visitation figures suffered. The show did give Detective Parton his due in solving the crimes. The damage had been done, however, and time was the only thing that could heal the wounds caused by these horrendous murders. In time, the wounds did heal and tranquility and confidence returned to the city of Gatlinburg.

Robbery and Murder at Family Inns East in Pigeon Forge

During the early morning hours of Wednesday, October 4, 2000, Pamela Hale, the night clerk at Family Inns East in Pigeon Forge was bludgeoned to death behind her desk and left lying on the floor in a pool of blood. The office and check-in counter had been ransacked and the cash drawers were missing. This scene was discovered by Wayne Knight, an evidence technician with the Pigeon Forge Police Department.

Later that afternoon, the missing cash drawers were located on the bank of the Little Pigeon River next to the northbound lanes on the Spur just south of Pigeon Forge. A

TBI crime lab technician dusted for and lifted identifiable latent fingerprints from the cash drawers. Over nine months later a positive match was made with the known fingerprints of Brandon Tipton. On July 13, 2001 Tipton furnished a signed statement to the Pigeon Forge Police implicating himself and his wife, Michelle Tipton, in the homicide and robbery. (On October 4, 2000 Brandon and Michelle were not married but lived together in Pigeon Forge; they married on October 5, 2000, the day following the murder.) Later that same day Michelle Tipton told the TBI and Pigeon Forge Police that she was not with Brandon on the evening of October 3, 2000. She confirmed she had returned home at about seven o'clock the following morning. That same evening Michelle called the Pigeon Forge Police Department and talked to Lieutenant Barbara Ward and told her that she had lied during her earlier statement and that she was, in fact, at home on the evening of October 3rd.

On the following day, July 14th, Michelle appeared at the Pigeon Forge Police Department asking about her husband's status. She was advised of her rights and was then shown her husband's statement taken the day before implicating her in the robbery and murder of Pamela Hale. After reading the first and part of the second page of her husband's statement, she admitted her involvement and furnished a signed statement of her own. The statements were in general agreement. They had driven to Gatlinburg that evening to burglarize the TCBY on Airport Road but decided against it after spotting a police officer nearby. Brandon had stolen a pair of bolt cutters from Walmart earlier the same day to use in the burglary.

Later that same evening they drove to Pigeon Forge and decided to rob the Family Inns East. After looking at a room with the desk clerk under the guise of renting it, they all returned to lobby where Brandon hit the clerk on the head several times with the bolt cutters he had concealed under his jacket. Brandon grabbed the cash drawers, and Michelle drove them to their apartment where they determined there was $500—$600 inside. They left the apartment and drove to the banks of the Little Pigeon River just outside of Pigeon Forge and threw the cash drawers in the river. Michelle said they then drove to Iron Mountain Road where Brandon threw the bolt cutters into the woods. Based on that information, Detective Tim Trentham, who took her statement, recovered the murder weapon.

This homicide, like the others described previously, was also particularly aggravated. Brandon Tipton admitted in his signed statement that … "I took the bolt cutters and struck her in the head at least 3 times. Once in the back of the head and one in the forehead. I don't know where else in the head I hit her." The medical examiner who performed the autopsy on Ms. Hale testified, however, that she had one blunt trauma injury to her forehead and fourteen blunt trauma injuries to the top of her head.

In February 2003 Brandon Tipton pled guilty to first degree murder and felony murder. He was sentenced to life in prison without the possibility of parole. In July of that same year Michelle Tipton went to trial and was convicted of felony murder and second degree murder. She was sentenced to two life sentences to run concurrently. On August 22, 2005 Michelle's conviction for second degree murder was reversed; her conviction for first degree felony murder and resulting sentencing was affirmed.

All Cases Prosecuted by Schmutzer

All of these murder cases, with the exception of the unsolved Teaster case, were prosecuted by Sevierville native Al Schmutzer, Jr., Attorney General for the Fourth Judicial District that includes Sevier, Cocke, Jefferson, and Grainger Counties for the 32 years between 1974 and 2006. He shares the same feelings of torment and frustration as Watson regarding the Teaster murders.

Schmutzer was a successful, aggressive, and highly respected prosecutor who personally handled the prosecution of numerous murder cases while in office. He was a strong proponent of sensible sentencing guidelines commensurate with the crime and a fierce defender of victims' rights. He was well-equipped to handle such cases having started his career as an FBI Agent in Boston and New York and later as a practicing attorney in Sevierville before being elected attorney general. Sevier County and the Fourth Judicial District will always be indebted to Schmutzer for his masterful handling of not only these cases, but all the cases that fell under his purview and tutelage during his tenure as Attorney General.

Chapter 17

The Author's Observations and Conclusions

During the seven or so years that the site of the Perry's Camp murders continued to stand following September 1949, I would always get "the willy's" every time I rode past. Even though I knew the feeling that would come over me, I would still always look. It was a one-of-a-kind spot in Sevier County with a one-of-a-kind meaning. It represented my first experience with unthinkable torture and felony murder. Like many young Sevier Countians, I had trouble understanding "the why" behind the crimes. And, also like others my age, it was something that stayed with me for the rest of life.

It was these feelings, the desire to re-establish the facts of the crimes that never aired at a public trial, and the need to try to understand the actions of Claude Robertson that drove me to gather the facts through research and interviews necessary to produce this non-fiction work. It was not intended to re-open old wounds, to hurt or tarnish any family's name, dead or living, or to air Sevier County's dirty laundry. It was a conscientious search for the truth about a significant event in the County's history.

I think that the careful reading of those chapters having to do with the investigation of the crimes and the testimony of Sheriff Roy Whaley should cause most readers to agree with my interpretation of the evidence and the time line of the crimes. There was some very pertinent evidence developed during the course of researching this subject that was not publicly exposed in 1949, either in the press or at the trial. I was unable to determine exactly how much of this evidence was known at the time and by whom. I think it is important to reveal and highlight the evidence now as it has bearing on motive, the acquittal of Basil Jones, and the decision not to proceed with a jury trial.

The motives differed for Robertson and the Jones brothers. For Robertson, his murder of Charlie Perry was a revenge killing; robbery was simply a fringe benefit. The money was a perk that allowed him to spend Perry's money for his personal pleasure. The money allowed him to buy a car, a very nice car that many would envy, a 1940 Ford, a Deluxe model with twin taillights. Bad blood had existed between Robertson and Perry for years. Perry had put Robertson out of his place more times than anyone could count. Perry suspected that Robertson had burned down his power house when Robertson was released from prison in early 1943 for the killing of "Bun" Ward. It is likely that Robertson learned that Perry had loaned $2,000 to the Ward family for his prosecution for the murder of "Bun" Ward. There may have been other reasons for the bad blood. One of Robertson's sisters suspected Claude had been in the liquor business with Perry and that they had had a falling out, however, no corroboration of this allegation was uncovered. This seems unlikely since Robertson did not have a car. To run illegal liquor without a car would have been inconvenient but not impossible.

Aside from the unsupported supposition by Claude's sister that Claude and Perry bootlegged together, there were other criminal associations developed suggesting a possible criminal connection between the two men. In 1934 Perry furnished information to the Knox County Sheriff's Office and/or the Knoxville Police Department resulting in the recovery of $15,000 worth of apparel taken during the burglary of American Clothing on Jackson Avenue in

Knoxville. The apparel was recovered from one of Perry's cabins and three members of the Ernie Miller Gang, a loosely-organized group of felons involved in various criminal activities, in particular, armed robberies, burglaries, and bootlegging, were charged and convicted. Buford Roberts, a known member of this gang, was arrested by the Knoxville Police immediately following the Perry murders under the theory the gang was possibly finally seeking revenge against Perry for informing on them 15 years earlier. Robertson was never directly tied to the Ernie Miller Gang, however, Mosey Moore, Robertson's crime partner, told his nephew, Jim Moore, Jr., that he and Robertson and two other men, one from Gatlinburg and one from Blount County, pulled several armed robberies together. Brownlee Reagan, former Tennessee Highway Patrolman and former Gatlinburg Chief of Police identified the same Gatlinburg resident as a suspect along with Ernie Miller in an armed robbery that occurred in Townsend during which the victim was hurt or even killed. Neither man was ever charged.

For the Jones, the motive was simple—money—but one of them, Hermie Lee, had to know the murders were going to occur. Perry was Robertson's target, not the Jones.' It was Robertson who was a Sevier County native and lived three miles from Perry's Camp. It was Robertson who had had problems with Perry, had been thrown out of his place, and had had disagreements with him. The Jones' were from Fall Branch in Washington County 76 miles away. They didn't know Perry or Josie Law. But Hermie Lee knew Claude Robertson. They had served federal time together at Terre Haute and Ashland two years before. He knew Robertson had killed before and that bad blood existed between Perry and Robertson. Hermie Lee Jones had to be told everything about Perry's Camp to know what to expect and to be able to carry out the robbery. These are the reasons that Hermie Lee Jones had to know that Charlie Perry was going to die that night and that Josie Law, if she was there, would also die. Both Charlie and Josie could and would have readily identified Claude Robertson to Sheriff Whaley.

The three men had driven past Perry's Camp the evening before but decided against committing the robbery that Sunday evening after spotting a car parked at the office. The following night with Basil driving Hermie Lee's Plymouth, Claude and Hermie Lee were dropped off nearby and walked the rest of the way. Claude had parked the car he was driving, the owner of which was undisclosed, a mile or so back down the road. There is no way to know how much Basil knew at this point about what was about to happen. He was the driver, the lookout. There wasn't any need for him know details, the relationship between Robertson and Perry, or anything else. Had Hermie Lee brought his little brother into a robbery conspiracy without telling him at least one murder, and maybe two, was going to occur? He may have. This would explain why Hermie Lee was willing to plead guilty to murder and accept a 99-year sentence in return for his kid brother to be set free.

Another significant piece of evidence that may or may not have been known to Sheriff Whaley, but which was not included in his testimony, was the identity of a laundry mark on a shirt collar found among the ashes and burned fragments of bloody clothes located on the Jones' property in Washington County. It may have been omitted from Whaley's testimony because he didn't know the identity of the person to whom the laundry mark belonged. Marion Robertson, Claude's father, knew. After learning the initials on the collar, he went to his daughter who lived in Knoxville and asked her about it. She told the former sheriff that Claude had been arrested in Knoxville for public drunkenness the week before the murders and had come to her house after being released from jail to get cleaned up. He spent the night and left the next day wearing her husband's shirt she had loaned him. The shirt's collar bore her laundry mark—her initials. It is not known if Claude's father furnished this information to Whaley; however, it seems unlikely that he did since Whaley made no mention of it during his testimony. This evidence was significant as it corroborated Robertson's statement to Sheriff Whaley and did so without Robertson having to testify. This shirt collar was more compelling evidence against the Jones' than Robertson's testimony would have been. It was entirely credible.

The revenge motive and the shirt collar would have arguably presented questions for a jury to answer about the involvement of Basil Jones. Had Hermie Lee hung his brother out to dry by allowing him to enter into the robbery conspiracy not knowing that it involved murder? The shirt collar would have raised another question for the jury. Where was Basil while Robertson and Hermie Lee were burning their blood-splattered clothes? Did he light the fire or was he inside the house in his bed asleep?

All these questions now make for interesting debate, but unfortunately, there is no one left alive to answer them.

After ferreting out the gruesome details of three murders—"Bun" Ward in 1940, and Josie Law and Charlie Perry in 1949—it appears that Claude Robertson may have committed a fourth murder during the commission of an armed robbery in early 1947. Mosey Moore, who admitted being scared to death of Robertson, told stories of armed robberies that he committed with Robertson to his nephew, James Moore, Jr., after Robertson was safely locked up in the Nashville penitentiary. Moore told his nephew about an armed robbery "up north" during which Robertson killed the victim. Robertson was under the impression or feared that Mosey was going to turn him in for that murder and that this was the reason Robertson was at the home of Hattie Moore Greene, his sister, when Robertson was arrested for the murders of Perry and Law on September 23, 1949.

Robertson had only been out of federal prison 50 days when he was arrested in front of Hattie Greene's house. He had been placed in federal custody to begin serving his sentence on May 31, 1947, two and one-half months after he was arrested for felonious assault in the near-death beating of Mosey Moore on Sutherland Avenue in Knoxville but only 25 days after that case was dismissed. Claude was after Mosey shortly before and shortly after his federal incarceration. It follows that the armed robbery-homicide Mosey related to his nephew most likely occurred during early 1947 when both Claude and Mosey were living and working in the Lonsdale area of Knoxville.

Finally, aside from childhood feelings and the desire to know what happened, the remaining reason for writing this book was Claude Robertson, my second cousin once removed. I summarized Claude's heritage at the beginning of Chapter 6 and pointed out that he was an exception. Why was he an exception? Why was he different from his forefathers and the rest of his family? Why was he a killer? Was Claude "chemically imbalanced?" Was he a psychotic or a psychopathic serial killer? Or, was he just plain mean?

Most everyone with whom Steve and I talked during the course of this quest who knew Claude characterized him as "just plain mean," or as "the meanest drunk you'd ever want to meet." Without question his drinking had a profound effect on his behavior. To suggest there was a "chemical imbalance" would be to use an over-used and somewhat obsolete term used to try to explain a personality, schizophrenia, or other psychotic disorder as the cause of his behavior. An alternative explanation from "just plain mean" and a psychotic disorder is serial killer.

There are two types of serial killers, a person who attacks and kills victims one by one in a series of incidents. The first type is a psychotic serial killer, one who is legally insane and cannot tell the difference between right and wrong. The second type, and the most prolific, is a psychopathic serial killer, one who knows the difference between right and wrong, but has no conscience and simply does not care that they are committing wrongful acts.

In the early 1970's the FBI established a "Behavioral Science Unit" at its Quantico, Virginia training academy. One of the agents in my training class became a member of this unit, and I utilized their expertise in field investigations during the late 1970's. Three agents in this unit, one of whom I heard speak at seminars and in-service training classes, interviewed 36 serial killers including "Son of Sam" David Berkowitz and Ted Bundy and compiled a list of fourteen general characteristics of serial killers.

No more than six of these fourteen characteristics formulated by the FBI even generally apply to Robertson. There is insufficient information available about Robertson's personal life to make any sort of determination about any other characteristics. The FBI also categorized serial killers by type and motive. Robertson does not fit into any of these defined categories.

Since the FBI conclusions in the 1970's many studies have been conducted in an effort to identify the reasons for multiple killings. One theory suggests that many murderers are the product of our violent society. Another theory suggests that a family environment that includes abuse and failure to establish a good relationship with male figures is likely to produce a serial killer. Another popular theory is that such a killer may have been rejected by his family after his repeated behavior of defiance, deceit, and threats that caused the family to grant him distance in order to maintain domestic peace. This theory of family isolation resulting from such threatening behavior may more closely fit Robertson than any other. There are also studies that suggest genetic make-up play a part in breeding serial killers. Studies are many, but clear, definitive findings are few, except for one. All researchers agree that one of the most common traits among serial killers is heavy use of alcohol.

After all that it appears those who knew Claude Robertson may have had it right from the beginning. Maybe Claude Robertson was "just plain mean" or, as some put it, "the meanest drunk you'd ever want to meet." These were words of Sevier Countians, but the most pointed adjectives used to describe Robertson were those typed by the prison evaluator at the Nashville penitentiary in September, 1951. He typed the words ... "bad man, cool, calculating, poor personality, cruel, insolent and uncooperative ... has no rationalization to offer for his crime, to which he plead guilty and states he is guilty."

The author's collaborator concurs totally with these observations and conclusions.